THE WAR TO END ALL WARS
THE STORY OF WORLD WAR I

JACK BATTEN

TUNDRA BOOKS

Published in Canada by Tundra Books,
75 Sherbourne Street, Toronto, Ontario M5A 2P9

Published in the United States by Tundra Books of Northern New York,
P.O. Box 1030, Plattsburgh, New York 12901

Library of Congress Control Number: 2008910105

Library and Archives Canada Cataloguing in Publication

Batten, Jack, 1932-
The war to end all wars : the story of WWI / Jack Batten.

Includes bibliographical references and index.
ISBN 978-0-88776-879-8

1. World War, 1914-1918 – Juvenile literature. I. Title.

D522.7.B38 2009   j940.3   C2008-907123-9

We acknowledge the financial support of the Government of Canada through the Book Publishing Industry Development Program (BPIDP) and that of the Government of Ontario through the Ontario Media Development Corporation's Ontario Book Initiative.

We further acknowledge the support of the Canada Council for the Arts and the Ontario Arts Council for our publishing program.

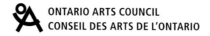

While every attempt for accuracy in the endpaper maps was made by the publisher, borders in 1914 were not clearly defined. We regret any error or omission.

Design: Andrew Roberts

Printed and bound in Canada

1 2 3 4 5 6   14 13 12 11 10 09

For the ever-helpful and gracious de Penciers

What passing-bells for these who die as cattle?
Only the monstrous anger of the guns.
From "Anthem for Doomed Youth"
by Wilfred Owen, 1917

CONTENTS

1 ONE BOY'S WAR

A FEW MINUTES BEFORE TWO O'CLOCK on the afternoon of October 12, 1916, Ray Goodyear began to fit the bayonet into his rifle. It was something he'd done so often in army drills that it had become almost automatic. But he fumbled the bayonet on that October afternoon. It wasn't a drill he was performing this time. He was about to go into his first-ever battle against the Germans.

Eighteen years old and promoted to lance corporal the month before, Ray served in the Newfoundland Regiment. As he finally pushed the bayonet into place, about nine hundred of his fellow Newfoundlanders and tens of thousands of British troops all around him crouched in long lines of trenches. They were waiting for the signal to attack the German positions near the village of Gueudecourt, in the Somme district of northern France.

Ray checked his bayonet again. Nervous, excited, and proud, he was as ready for war as a boy could be.

Lance Corporal Ray Goodyear fought the Germans for the first time at the Battle of the Somme. Ray had just turned eighteen. (David Macfarlane)

———

A year earlier, Ray had been working in the horse stables back home in Grand Falls, a mill town in Newfoundland's northern interior. Four of his five older brothers – Joe, Stan, Ken, and Hedley – joined up as soon as the war that everyone was calling the Great War broke out in Europe, in early August of 1914. They were fighting overseas when Ray was still in high school. He talked about his brothers all the time and said he could hardly wait to follow them to Europe.

Twice, when Ray was still seventeen – a year too young to volunteer for service without his parents' permission – he ran away to Port aux Basques, in Newfoundland's far southwest corner. It was a distant town where nobody knew Ray, where he could try to get away with lying about his age and joining the army. Both times, Ray's father, Josiah, figured out what the boy was up to. Josiah caught the train to Port aux Basques and dragged his son back to Grand Falls.

But Ray was stubborn. Day after day, he made his case for enlistment to his father. In the spring of 1916, Josiah gave in. Though Ray was still a few weeks short of eighteen, Josiah allowed him to sign on with the Newfoundland Regiment. The youngest Goodyear would join his brothers on Europe's battlefields.

Newfoundlanders hated it when soldiers from Britain, France, and the other countries on the Allied side in the war mistook them for Canadians. Newfoundland was an independent Dominion in those days, long before it became a province of Canada in 1949. Small and poor, its total population under two hundred thousand, Newfoundland showed its loyalty to Britain and the Empire by sending almost six thousand soldiers to the war.

In the summer of 1916, Ray Goodyear and the rest of the new recruits from Newfoundland were in training at Britain's military grounds on the Salisbury Plain, in the south of England. They learned how to march, shoot, and obey orders.

After three months of drills, they traveled across the English Channel to a camp outside the ancient walled city of Ypres, in northwest Belgium. Ray was now on the Western Front, where Allied and German troops had been fighting one another since the first months of the war.

Ypres felt quiet at the time Ray arrived. But not long before, it and the surrounding area had been the scene of horrific battles. The bodies of soldiers killed in the shooting and shelling still lay in the fields. Ray's stomach lurched at the sight. They were the first dead people he had ever seen.

In the French village of Hangest-en-Santerre, close to the fighting in the Battle of the Somme, a drummer girl reads an official proclamation warning citizens of approaching German troops. The grinning French soldiers in the background don't appear to be taking the proclamation seriously. (ILN/Mary Evans Picture Library)

In the second week of October, the Newfoundlanders rode buses from Ypres to the Somme, where they joined British troops for the attack near Gueudecourt. The nine hundred men of the Newfoundland Regiment would go into battle as a unit, alongside the tens of thousands of British infantrymen.

This was to be a crucial fight. Allied soldiers in the hundreds of thousands had been killed since Britain launched the Battle of the Somme on July 1. The sacrifice of all those men hadn't brought victory; nothing the Allies had done came close to driving the Germans into retreat. It was too soon to call the Battle of the Somme a total failure, but Britain badly needed success at Gueudecourt.

In the early afternoon of October 12, the British artillery began firing shells high across the empty fields toward the German lines. The shelling followed a pattern that the British hadn't tried before. The generals called it a creeping barrage.

Gunners blasted salvos of shells, paused to reset the guns, aimed the next bombardment fifty yards further on, and fired again. They repeated the operation over and over, always increasing the range by fifty yards.

As the shells flew overhead, the Allied infantrymen advanced out of the trenches and into the fields, keeping just behind the moving curtains of artillery fire. Their orders were to proceed steadily – not fast enough to overtake the barrage and not slow enough to get far behind their fellow soldiers.

According to the theory of the creeping barrage, the Germans would be so busy dodging the falling shells that they couldn't give any serious trouble to the attacking Allied soldiers.

Ray Goodyear and his Newfoundland comrades climbed onto the battlefield. An army regulation that seems strange to us today required every man to carry sixty-five pounds of equipment on his back. Like each of his fellow soldiers, Ray was loaded down with a rifle, 170 rounds of ammunition, a water bottle, food rations, a first-aid kit, two sandbags, two hand grenades, a waterproof cape, a small spade, and a pair of wire cutters. Under this burden, Ray covered the ground not much faster than at a slow trot.

The racket of the big guns blotted out all other sounds on the battlefield. If Ray's officers called out orders, he couldn't be sure he heard them. And it was hard to see through the thick smoke and dust that clouded the air. Shells had churned the earth into such an uneven mess that Ray needed to concentrate on keeping his balance. He had to make his way forward largely on feel and instinct.

Canadian troops charge from their trenches during the last days of the fighting at the Somme. (ILN/Mary Evans Picture Library)

The creeping barrage, which the British officers considered such a clever strategy, proved to be a long way short of perfection. At several points along the line of advance, soldiers grew anxious and impatient. They pressed ahead too quickly. The men in the rear forced those in front into the path of shells from their own artillery. Sometimes artillery gunners made miscalculations and aimed short. Their shells hit advancing soldiers from behind. It was estimated that slightly more than one-tenth of the Allied troops who died at Gueudecourt were killed by the guns of the creeping barrage.

As Ray Goodyear moved across the battlefield, a captain from the regiment fell in step to his left. For a short time, the two kept the same deliberate pace. That was how it happened that the captain caught a glimpse of Ray at the moment Ray seemed to trip, his arms flung forward, an expression of surprise on his face.

Thinking Ray had stumbled on a piece of broken earth, the captain paused to help him back to his feet. But, glancing down, the captain realized the real reason for Ray's fall – a piece of shell had hit him in the stomach, tearing out his insides. Death had brought the look of surprise to Ray's face.

Whether the shell that killed Ray came from the German lines or from the British creeping barrage, no other soldier could later swear to a certainty. Ray's family never learned whose shell brought about his death.

By the finish of the fighting on the late afternoon of October 12, the Newfoundland Regiment had captured six hundred yards of enemy territory. The Germans that they beat back were no pushovers. These German soldiers were so tough that their own people named them the Iron Division. But the Iron Division couldn't match the men from Newfoundland on this day.

The six hundred yards carried the Newfoundlanders only halfway to the objective that the generals had set for their unit that day. But their advance still drove deeper into enemy lines than any other Allied troops managed at the same time. The Newfoundlanders killed 250 Germans and took seventy-five prisoners. One hundred and twenty of the Newfoundland Regiment's own men died in the Gueudecourt attack, and another 119 suffered wounds.

Ray wasn't the only Goodyear brother killed in the war. In 1917, on the Western Front, a German shell struck Stan Goodyear. He died on the spot. A year later, again on the Western Front, a German sniper shot Hedley Goodyear in the head, killing him in an instant.

Three Goodyears gave their lives, but Ray was the first and the youngest. As his sister remembered him later, "He was just a boy." Ray had been so eager to measure up to his older brothers. Just like them, he would shoot his gun and defeat the enemy. In the end, as far as anyone could tell, he never had the chance to fire his rifle. When he got his turn to fight the Germans, his time on the battlefield lasted no more than fifteen minutes.

When Ray joined the Newfoundland Regiment, he understood that the Germans were the evil enemy that must be beaten. In his own mind, he didn't need to know any more, and the origins of the war remained a mystery to him. He couldn't have answered the deeper questions: *Why were millions of men killing one another? What brought nations into such terrible conflict with other nations? What started the Great War?*

Ray Goodyear, dead at eighteen, wouldn't have known.

2 THE PATH TO CATASTROPHE

FOR A MAN WHO HELD ENORMOUS POWER, Kaiser Wilhelm II of Germany had a thin skin. The kaiser – the title for a German emperor – ruled all of the German people. In the early twentieth century, no nation surpassed his in industrial strength and military might.

In appearance, the kaiser seemed perfect for his emperor's role. He was always smartly turned out in a crisp uniform, and he trimmed his mustache so that it turned defiantly upwards at each end. Despite his look of authority, the kaiser was easily insulted, the most innocent remark sending him into a rage. When he compared himself and his countrymen with the French or the British, what he felt most often was envy and frustration.

It drove the kaiser crazy that France hadn't once invited him to visit Paris. The city was the universal center of the arts, celebrated for its beauty, style, and architecture. But the kaiser had never set foot on Paris's grand avenue, the Champs Élysées, nor

Formidable in expression, mustache, and uniform, Kaiser Wilhelm II of Germany believed that the twentieth century belonged to his country, even if it took a war to prove it. (ILN/Mary Evans Picture Library)

gazed up at its magnificent Eiffel Tower. While the French might fear Germany, they didn't give the kaiser and his people an ounce of respect. France regarded German culture as crude compared to its own, and the French had long and painful memories of Germany's crushing victory over them in the brief war of 1870.

In the kaiser's opinion, Britain's treatment of his country was even worse. Britain's rich nobility rarely bothered to include Germany on their tours of the continent. They behaved as if the country hardly existed. The kaiser took every imagined British slight personally because he was related by birth to Britain's royal family. His mother was the eldest child of the nine sons and daughters born to Queen Victoria, who reigned over Great Britain and its Empire from 1837 until her death in 1901.

The family relations not only made the kaiser a grandson to Victoria, but also a nephew to Edward VII, who followed Victoria to the British throne, and a cousin to George V, who became king after Edward died in 1910. These connections were intimate, and yet, in the years since Wilhelm II succeeded to the title of kaiser in 1888, he and his country never received the recognition from Britain that he thought a sovereign of his stature deserved a thousand times over.

Germany's philosophers had been writing for years that Germans were inherently superior people. The country's most famous philosopher, Friedrich Nietzsche, called his fellow Germans "supermen." To their core, Germans regarded themselves as more developed in mind, body, and spirit than other races and nationalities. They were certain that the twentieth century would belong to them and that they would finally demonstrate their supremacy to the world.

The possibility that Germany's national ego might lead to war didn't bother the country's military leaders. One of them, General Friedrich von Bernhardi, wrote a book in 1911 in which he looked forward to the prospect of warfare.

He called war "a biological necessity." He said that Germany had a choice between world power and its own disintegration. To Bernhardi's way of thinking, this was no choice at all: Germany had a moral duty to impress its superiority on the rest of the world. If war was necessary to accomplish the objective, then that was the direction history must take.

——

In preparation for war, the German Army had a secret plan for victory. It was called the Schlieffen Plan, named after the general who'd tinkered at it for years until he was satisfied the plan had the fewest possible chances for error.

General Alfred von Schlieffen held the post of chief of the German General Staff from 1891 until his retirement in 1906. Even with the playful monocle that Schlieffen wore in one eye, his natural expression looked fierce. Single-minded, he devoted all of his time to the army and to his plan. Schlieffen's idea of relaxation at the end of a long day spent over his calculations was to read to his daughters from books on military history.

Convinced that a war against France, Germany's major rival on the continent, and likely Russia as well would happen one day, Schlieffen came up with a scheme for knocking out both countries in a hurry.

He committed seven-eighths of Germany's army of almost one and a half million soldiers to the capture of Paris in exactly six weeks. With the fall of Paris, Schlieffen thought all of France would fall to its knees. In the meantime, during those crucial six weeks, the other one-eighth of the German Army was assigned to hold off Russia in the east.

The genius of Schlieffen's plan, in his view, lay in the route that the army would take in its attack on France. While a smaller force would advance along the obvious path straight west across the border between Germany and France, the great mass of German infantry would enter France unexpectedly, by way of its frontier with Belgium. The German soldiers were to make a gigantic sweep north and west from Germany into Belgium. Then they would drive south through Belgium, cross the Belgian-French border, and push on into Paris.

At the end of the sixth week, the moment France was crushed, most of the conquering army would rush by troop trains several hundred miles to the east. Once there, the Germans would inflict a similar beating on Russia.

In the early 1900s, the other European countries kept on close watch for German treachery.

France had been particularly attentive ever since Germany's quick victory in the 1870 war between the two countries. After that triumph, the Germans made two demands to punish the defeated French: one was payment of a gigantic fine of five billion francs, and the other was the handing over to Germany of Alsace-Lorraine, a prosperous French territory bordering Germany.

France intended never to experience such humiliation again. As one protection against another German invasion, it arranged a military alliance with Russia in 1892. Under the alliance's terms, if Germany attacked either France or Russia, both countries would declare war on the Germans.

As for Great Britain, its fondest wish was to avoid getting mixed up in any alliance with the continental countries. At this, it was largely successful.

But Germany's navy made the British nervous. Britain had ruled the seas for hundreds of years, with the most powerful navy known to mankind. As an island kingdom, it depended on the navy for its first and best line of defense. Now, as the world moved into the twentieth century, the Germans had amassed a naval force second in size only to Britain's. The British expected that, one day, they would need to confront the kaiser's fleet.

The single significant agreement that Britain signed with continental countries dated all the way back to 1839. In the early 1830s, Belgium was created as an independent nation. Since Belgium lay a relatively short distance across the English Channel from England's coast, Britain wanted to protect the new nation against invasion by any country that might be unfriendly to the British.

Britain negotiated the Treaty of London, guaranteeing Belgium's independence and neutrality. Britain and France signed the treaty. If any nation invaded Belgium, then the invader would have to answer to Britain and France.

By the early 1900s, the only invader that the British and the French could imagine was Germany. Though Britain and France had no knowledge of the secret Schlieffen Plan, if Germany should ever activate it, the plan would set off the 1839 treaty.

———

Perhaps Europe's most civilized monarch, King Albert I of Belgium takes a lead in opposing Germany's threats. He is shown here with his wife, Queen Elisabeth, and their children – Princess Marie-José, Prince Charles, and Prince Léopold. (ILN/Mary Evans Picture Library)

Germany's one good friend in Europe was the Austro-Hungarian Empire. Worn and rickety, the least of the European powers, the Empire nevertheless covered a tremendously large territory in central Europe. Besides Austria and Hungary, it included most of the Balkan countries on the coast of the Adriatic Sea to the south.

The Habsburgs, a centuries-old German family dynasty, ruled over Austria-Hungary, but the ruling wasn't easy. The difficulty lay in the wide variations in backgrounds of the Empire's citizens: among them were five major religions and twelve national groups. Not all of these differing people were happy with their Habsburg masters.

The citizens of Serbian blood especially resisted Habsburg domination. Living in Bosnia-Herzegovina, the Balkan region annexed by the Empire in 1908, the Serbs desperately wanted release from Austria-Hungary.

Freedom would let them join with their brothers in Serbia, a small but ferocious kingdom next door to Bosnia. Serbia stirred up trouble by giving the Bosnian Serbs plenty of encouragement in resisting the Empire's authority. Not surprisingly, Serbia's interference angered the Austro-Hungarians, who would welcome the day when their army could squash the upstart little country.

The only reason for Austria-Hungary to hold its fire against Serbia was the close Russian relationship with the Serbs. Russia regarded Serbia as the junior friend they were bound to protect. The size of Russia's army, potentially six million strong, made the Austro-Hungarians uneasy. As a precaution, the Empire negotiated an arrangement with Germany guaranteeing that the Germans would support Austria-Hungary if it should get into a disagreement with Russia.

All of the European countries were committed to alliances and treaties that could plunge them into war with one or more of the others if the right circumstances came along. Each nation was like a cache of dynamite waiting for someone to put a match to it. But where might the spark come from that would ignite the countries in battle?

Years earlier, Prince Otto von Bismarck had an answer. Bismarck, who died in 1898, was the wisest German politician of the nineteenth century. Near the end of his life, he suggested what could bring about warfare in modern Europe: "Some damned foolish thing in the Balkans."

3 THE SPARK THAT LIT THE FIRE

IN THE SPRING OF 1914, a nineteen-year-old Bosnian Serb named Gavrilo Princip learned he had tuberculosis. Despite the disease, Princip joined in a plot designed by a radical nationalist group in Serbia called the Black Hand Society. The plot involved the assassination of Archduke Franz Ferdinand – the nephew of Emperor Franz Josef of the Austro-Hungarian Empire and the heir to the throne.

Members of the Black Hand thought the assassination would show the Empire that they meant business in demanding the right of their fellow Serbs in Bosnia to break free from the Austro-Hungarians and join Serbia. Gavrilo Princip agreed to take part in the murder with five other young men. He felt he had nothing to lose: he was dying of TB anyway.

On the morning of June 28, Franz Ferdinand arrived in Sarajevo, the capital city of Bosnia, having completed his duties as the official observer of the annual Austro-Hungarian military maneuvers. He and his wife, Duchess Sophie, rode in

The assassination on June 28, 1914, of this man, Austro-Hungarian Archduke Franz Ferdinand, plunges the nations into war. (Toronto Reference Library)

a motorcade from Sarajevo's train station to the town hall, where the mayor was waiting to greet them. Franz Ferdinand insisted on an open convertible so that he could show off his beautiful Sophie to the welcoming crowd.

Stationed at different spots along the motorcade's advertised route were Princip and his fellow assassins. One of the young men, not Princip, threw a hand grenade at the archduke's convertible. The grenade bounced off the car's folded-down top and landed under the next car in the line. When the grenade exploded, it wounded two army officers inside the second car.

The archduke's convertible, untouched, sped away to the town hall, where Franz Ferdinand made an angry speech about the violence of his reception. After the town hall ceremony, Franz Ferdinand changed his plans for the day: rather than pass along the route that was intended to take his motorcade out of Sarajevo, he and his party would drive to the local hospital for a visit with the officers injured in the grenade attack.

But nobody told the archduke's chauffeur about the new arrangement. He set off on the original route, until someone at last ordered him to switch course for the hospital. At that moment, the convertible was on Franz Josef Avenue, a street named after the reigning emperor. The archduke's chauffeur stopped the car and began to back out of Franz Josef. By the worst possible luck for the archduke, Gavrilo Princip happened to be sitting in a delicatessen on that very street.

Princip knew of the failed grenade attack. Thinking the assassination plans were on hold, he dropped into Schiller's Delicatessen for a sandwich. Schiller's was on the motorcade's route, but Princip was astounded to see the archduke's convertible, still with the top down, appear on Franz Josef Avenue.

Princip ran out of the delicatessen, a pistol in his hand. He fired at Franz Ferdinand first, then at Sophie. Princip was so close, and his targets were so exposed in the open car, that his shots could hardly miss. One bullet struck the archduke in his neck, and another hit Sophie in her abdomen. The convertible hurried to the nearby Bosnian governor's residence for medical help.

The archduke dismissed his wound as of no consequence, saying more than once that it was nothing. These words, in which he badly misdiagnosed his own injuries, were the last he spoke. Franz Ferdinand and Sophie died that afternoon.

Gavrilo Princip was captured at the scene of the assassinations. He was sent to prison, where he died in 1918 of tuberculosis.

The frowning young man in the center is Gavrilo Princip, photographed not long after he is arrested for the shooting death of the heir to the Austro-Hungarian throne, Archduke Franz Ferdinand. (Toronto Reference Library)

Outraged by the murder of the heir to their throne, the Austro-Hungarians were all in favor of an immediate invasion of Serbia. First, however, they wanted reassurance that Germany would support their action.

In these and other negotiations, nothing much happened right away. It was summer, and in European capitals, leaders weren't available to hold discussions or make decisions. They had left on their annual holidays.

In Germany, the kaiser boarded the royal yacht and sailed off on a three-week cruise through the Norwegian fjords. He couldn't be reached. For part of the month, President Raymond Poincaré of France and his prime minister, René Viviani, were also at sea, traveling to and from a state visit in Russia.

In Belgrade, the capital of Serbia, where foreign representatives needed to exercise diplomacy if a war between the Serbs and the Austro-Hungarians was to be headed off, the key officials were out of commission. The British representative fell sick. The Russian representative had recently died and hadn't yet been replaced. The French representative suffered a nervous breakdown. Maybe the poor Frenchman saw a larger war looming, and the very thought overwhelmed him.

In the last week of July, events began to pave the way to disaster.

On Tuesday, July 28, with Germany's pledge of support, Austria-Hungary declared war on Serbia. The next day, it shelled Belgrade. On the same day, July 29, Russia positioned hundreds of thousands of army troops along its border with Austria, apparently ready to pounce. Two days later, July 31, Germany warned Russia that it must demobilize its army. The Germans gave the Russians twelve hours to respond to the ultimatum, a period that would end at noon on August 1.

On the afternoon of July 31, while Russia was thinking over the German demand, the kaiser stood on the balcony of his palace in Berlin and delivered a speech to tens of thousands of cheering Germans. Wearing an immaculate field-gray army uniform, he told his subjects that Germany was mobilizing its army for war.

In the speech, the kaiser talked of envy, but it wasn't his envy of Britain and France. He was speaking of the rest of the world's jealousy of Germany's natural superiority.

"A fateful hour has fallen upon Germany," he said, his voice rising. "Envious people on all sides are compelling us to resort to a just defense. The sword is being forced into our hands."

Saturday noon, August 1, came and went without a Russian answer to the German ultimatum. Later that afternoon, Germany declared war on Russia.

The declaration triggered Russia's 1892 treaty with France. Since the Russians were now at war with the Germans, the French were committed to join in the battle against them. France hesitated, not because it intended to back out of the treaty, but because it wanted to know Britain's position. The French couldn't resist Germany's behemoth of an army all by themselves. They needed Britain.

Britain made the French and everybody else wait. While its interests were with France, the British government refused to get mixed up in the continent's troubles unless the old 1839 treaty obliged it to act. Under the treaty, Britain promised to protect Belgium's independence and neutrality. So far, the Germans had made no threatening moves on the Belgians.

As this recruiting billboard in Toronto indicates, Canada's army wasn't above minor emotional blackmail in drawing men into the service of their country. (City of Toronto Archives, Fonds 1244, Item 724)

That situation changed at seven o'clock on Sunday evening, August 2, when Germany delivered a note to the Belgian government asking it to stand aside while the German Army marched through Belgium on its way to the French border. The note said that the Germans needed an answer within twelve hours. What went unmentioned was that Germany's soldiers would stomp across Belgium even if the country refused to open its borders voluntarily.

In a personal telegram to Belgium's King Albert, the kaiser encouraged Albert not to resist Germany. The kaiser ended the telegram by insisting that he wrote "only with the most friendly intentions toward Belgium."

"What does he take me for?" Albert burst out, angry at the hypocrisy.

King Albert was Europe's most civilized monarch. Comparatively young for a king at just thirty-nine, he was vigorous and intellectual. He liked reading books as much as he liked riding horses. He had common sense and tact.

The king needed both qualities on the night of August 2, when he called an emergency session with his country's military and government leaders. Working into the early hours of August 3, the king and his advisors thrashed out a response to Germany's ultimatum. Belgium was modestly sized in both land and population, but its people worked with exceptional industry, and the country thrived. Nobody at the meeting wanted to sacrifice Belgian prosperity, but neither did they care to cave in to the threatening Germans.

In the end, taking the lead from their sensible king, the Belgians declared that they wouldn't call Britain and France to their aid under the 1839 treaty unless Germany violated Belgium's border. Then the Belgians rejected the German request for free access to their country.

Germany received Belgium's answer at precisely seven o'clock Monday morning, August 3. Not happy with the response, but not surprised either, the Germans massed their troops along the Belgian border in preparation for the invasion of King Albert's little country.

By late afternoon of that Monday, France was frantic. Germany had declared war on the French a few hours earlier, and the German Army stood ready to attack Belgium. At this tense moment in international relations, France wanted desperately to know when Britain would stop dithering and join in the opposition to the German advance.

———

Britain tried one last diplomatic effort to resolve the frightening buildup to war. On Monday evening, it delivered an ultimatum to Germany demanding that the Germans halt their military operations against Belgium. Britain granted Germany twenty-four hours to comply.

The Germans had to laugh at the British note. They were on a roll to battle: nothing would stop them now. They didn't bother to answer the feeble ultimatum.

As the clock moved toward midnight on the following day – Tuesday, August 4 – Britain was left with only one choice. Diplomacy hadn't worked.

At midnight, Britain, Russia, and a much-relieved France were at war with Germany. Britain's declaration committed most of its Dominions and colonies to the war. Included among these Empire countries were Canada and Newfoundland. The Austro-Hungarian Empire soon took their expected place alongside Germany.

So it was that the Great War began.

4 FIRST BLOOD

MOST EVENINGS, GENERAL HELMUTH VON MOLTKE played his cello. When he had spare time, he liked to paint landscapes in watercolors. He was devoted to Christian Science, a religious movement that an American woman named Mary Baker Eddy started in the 1860s. Moltke didn't seem much like a typical hard-core German general.

But in the German Army of 1914, nobody outranked Moltke, and nobody was more excited about Germany's military destiny. Moltke had been the senior deputy to General von Schlieffen during the last two years of Schlieffen's term as chief of the German General Staff. When Schlieffen retired in 1906, Moltke became the new chief.

Moltke didn't mind that Schlieffen, in retirement, still came into the office to refine his famous plan for German victory. Few generals matched Moltke's enthusiasm for the Schlieffen Plan. He valued its perfect arrangement of troop train schedules, attack outlines, and number of miles of enemy territory to be captured in each day's fighting.

Calm and steady, French General Joseph Joffre takes charge of his nation's defense when the Germans strike a few miles from Paris in September 1914. (ILN/Mary Evans Picture Library)

In the midsummer of 1914, Moltke grew impatient to unleash the plan in the field. Finally, on the bright early morning of August 4 – many hours before Britain declared war – he gave the order for the German Army to begin crossing Belgium's frontier.

For the Belgian assault, Moltke had thirty-six infantry divisions to work with. At twenty thousand soldiers per division, the numbers represented a gargantuan army of 720,000 infantrymen plus cavalry, artillery, and supply wagons. A force larger than the population of most European cities was about to descend on little Belgium.

The thirty-six divisions were split among three armies, each commanded in the field by its own general. The First Army would invade from the far right, on a looping path that would enter France at the most western point of attack. Since the First Army had the longest march ahead of it – more than two hundred miles – the other two armies adjusted their advance to its pace. The Second Army's assignment was to cut directly down the center of Belgium, and the Third Army's job was to follow the most easterly and shortest route. All three German armies would converge as they got closer to Paris and victory.

To oppose the German colossus, King Albert could put up an army of just eighty thousand men. Not accustomed to war, Belgium's soldiers fought with antiquated rifles and little else. Still, while the Belgians were short on manpower and weapons, they felt fired up by patriotism and passion. In the first five days of the German invasion, Belgium's soldiers surprised everyone by performing so valiantly in the border fighting that they brought the mighty German Army to a momentary standstill.

King Albert thought the twelve Belgian forts at the city of Liège, twenty miles inside the border, would further slow the German advance. The forts, which controlled the major route through the rest of the country, were the one up-to-date element in the Belgian arsenal. Built deep into the ground, with little more than their heavy guns showing above the surface, the forts' construction was supposed to make it impossible for artillery attacks to damage them.

But King Albert didn't know about the new Krupp 420. It was Germany's secret weapon, the biggest gun in the world. Developed under utmost security, the gun measured twenty-four feet long, weighed ninety-eight tons, and had the ability to fire 2,000-pound shells over a range of nine miles. The Germans had no plan to bring the gun into action in the march through Belgium, but King Albert's resistance forced them to change tactics. They wheeled the Krupp 420 into position to blow away the foolish Belgians.

The gun's first target was Fort Pontisse. Once the gunners found the range, the 420 reduced Pontisse to dust and rubble. The Belgians couldn't believe the power of the shelling. It was as if a thousand ordinary howitzers fired all at once. The 420 blasted more of the Liège forts to smithereens until only two of the original twelve remained intact. Faced with the irrepressible gun, the last two forts surrendered.

Once past Liège, the three German armies swung into their march through Belgium. Only occasional rearguard raids by the Belgian Army hindered the advance. Aside from this irritation, the Germans in the field felt they were finding their stride.

General Moltke wasn't so sure.

In the west German city of Coblenz, where he set up his General Staff headquarters, Moltke studied the maps showing the positions of the three armies. Then he compared the positions with the calculations of the Schlieffen Plan. Above all, the advance that was intended to win the war in the shortest imaginable time must stick to the plan. It was essential that the Germans reach Paris in six weeks, before the French and British could organize their opposition to the attack, before Russia could fully mobilize its massive army in the east.

But as Moltke judged the situation on the maps, he realized that the Belgian resistance had cost his armies precious time and that the Germans hadn't traveled as deeply into Belgium as the plan called for at this stage. According to Moltke's figures, the German advance was two full days behind the Schlieffen Plan's schedule.

A small seed of doubt planted itself in Moltke's mind.

In the first two and a half weeks of the German push through Belgium, France sent no troops to cut off the enemy attack. General Joseph Joffre, chief of the French General Staff, didn't yet appreciate the strength of the German force coming at him from the north. Besides, Joffre had another priority: he wanted to take back the former French territory of Alsace-Lorraine. He sent his most battle-ready troops to carry out the assignment.

After an early brief success, the French troops were beaten into retreat by the Germans. The same thing happened when Joffre ordered another attack through the Ardennes region, northwest of Alsace-Lorraine. After these setbacks, it was past mid-August, and Joffre finally realized the threat of the tremendous German Army descending its way through Belgium.

On August 21, Joffre's French soldiers made the first German contact on Belgian soil near the town of Charleroi, just north of the France-Belgium border. Nine

As French troops march to battle in northern France's Champagne country, life goes on for the workers picking grapes. (ILN/Mary Evans Picture Library)

French divisions unexpectedly ran into three German divisions from the Second Army. Despite their advantage in numbers, the French once again found themselves on the losing end, and after two days of hard fighting, Joffre ordered his men back into France.

A dozen miles southwest of Charleroi, in the neighborhood of a Belgian mining town named Mons, the troops of the British Expeditionary Force had their first

The French soldier on the left has just been hit by a German bullet during fighting in the forest of Champenoux. (ILN/Mary Evans Picture Library)

taste of battle. It was August 23, and eighty thousand British soldiers had landed in French ports since August 9. On the move through northern France, they were asked by Joffre to take on Germany's immense First Army, which was heading south unaware that the British had arrived.

The British soldiers were career army men, hardened in the Boer War against South Africa fifteen years earlier. They marched into Belgium and took up position along twenty miles of the canal that ran through Mons. As the Germans came into range, the British opened up with their marvelous new Lee-Enfield rifles.

The Lee-Enfields fired so fast, at a clip of fifteen rounds a minute, that the Germans thought every British soldier must be equipped with a machine gun. Caught by surprise, the Germans desperately fought back. In the battle, which continued into the evening of the 23rd, the Germans lost five thousand men compared to just sixteen hundred for the British. On that day, it was Britain's victory, but the German First Army was so monumental in size that a one-day success was the best the BEF could hope for.

On August 24, the British followed the French in their retreat into northern France. By the last week of the month, all of the troops under Joffre's control, French and British, were showing their backs to the invading Germans.

General Joffre remained calm and unruffled. He was a short man, with a bushy white mustache and a bulging stomach. Even in the middle of war, he insisted on a good French lunch with wine each day and an even grander dinner. At night, he slept soundly. His confidence never deserted him, and in retreat, he saw a strategy for success.

"Our object must be to last out," he told his staff on August 24. "We will try to wear the enemy down and resume the offensive when the time comes."

Joffre's plan for turning retreat into eventual attack made sense. The German soldiers had been marching fifteen to twenty miles a day for almost four weeks. The broiling hot August sun was taking its toll on them. Frequently they got too far ahead of their supply wagons, and the men missed meals.

The retreating French and British troops halted now and again for a few hours of furious counterattacks. These sudden gun battles kept the Germans on edge. Fatigue and anxiety wore at them, creating conditions that worked in Joffre's favor.

The Joffre strategy got another boost from an unexpected source. Joffre's German counterpart, General Moltke, gave signs that the small doubts he felt earlier about the Schlieffen Plan's success might be growing into a full-blown loss of confidence.

In late August, he ordered several thousand troops to detach from his attacking force and leave for Russia. According to the Schlieffen Plan, the extra Germans wouldn't yet be needed in the east, but Moltke's nerve was faltering. He took more German soldiers out of the advance to deal with King Albert's soldiers, who were making fresh trouble for the Germans in Belgium's north. When Moltke was finished moving around his troops, he had reduced the German force attacking France by one-seventh.

Though the Schlieffen Plan virtually guaranteed victory, Moltke was stripping away its strengths. His most damaging move came when the three German armies moved closer to Paris, within thirty miles of the city, on September 5. In Schlieffen terms, it was the plan's thirty-sixth day: a time when Paris's fall to the Germans should come within the week. At this key point, Moltke's nerve slipped another notch, and in his anxious state, he let the armies get away from the alignment that Schlieffen designed.

His failure to instruct and control his commanders in the field opened a gap of thirty-five miles between the First and Second armies. They were supposed to present a solid front, but the two armies were drifting apart.

When the gap made the Germans vulnerable to a counterattack, Joffre chose to take his stand. He turned from defense to offense. After weeks of retreat, he ordered his troops to attack.

For three days, from September 6 to 9, Joffre threw everything he had at the Germans. Thirty French divisions plus five and a half British divisions brought tremendous intensity to the fight. They weren't equal to the German invaders in numbers nor in battlefield savvy, but they made up for the disadvantages with what the French called élan – spirit and a never-say-die attitude. Fighting on French ground, they would give their all.

Everything about the French attitude showed how eager they were for battle. When six thousand soldiers were stuck in Paris, with no transportation to take them thirty-five miles to the battlefields, a general named Clergerie comman-

Near the Belgian city of Ypres in the spring of 1915, British soldiers lie in wait for the Germans, seen along the horizon, to draw close before they fire. (ILN/Mary Evans Picture Library)

deered six hundred of the city's taxicabs. Each cab, carrying five soldiers per trip, drove twice from Paris to the battlefields and back again.

The six thousand men were thrilled to join their comrades in time to fight the Germans. The cab drivers were ecstatic to play their role in defending the country. This, everybody said, was real French élan.

On September 10, after three days of fierce clashes, the Germans chose to retreat. The decision came far too early. Still an exceptionally strong force, the German armies had Paris in sight. Even with the French waging the battle of their lives,

When British soldiers catch a German spy in their midst during the fighting in France in the autumn of 1914, they lose no time in carrying out his punishment. (ILN/Mary Evans Picture Library)

the Germans stood a good chance of taking the city. They could have ended the war there and then.

But Moltke was slow and indecisive in relaying his instructions from headquarters, and field commanders misread the situation on the ground. Almost by default, without a clear plan to oppose the gallant French, the German armies elected to go into reverse. They fell back along 350 miles of their front with the French and the British.

In Berlin, the kaiser was dumbfounded. He had been counting the days until Paris would be at his feet. Now this maddening Moltke, this cello-playing Christian Scientist, had botched the Schlieffen Plan.

On September 14, the kaiser took away Moltke's command, replacing him with Germany's minister of war, General Erich von Falkenhayn.

Falkenhayn was on the same wavelength as the kaiser. "Only one thing is certain," he had written in his diary on September 5. "Our General Staff has completely lost its head."

Moltke was gone, but Germany no longer had the chances that the Schlieffen Plan promised. The Germans were left with no choice: they had to change the way they had been fighting the war.

As the German armies took up their new positions on the high ground behind the Aisne River, northeast of Paris, they turned to trench warfare.

In military maneuvers over the previous decade, the German generals gave trenches a prominent place in their strategy. They taught the soldiers how to dig trenches in long winding lines, how to set up communications between trenches, how to use trenches as jumping-off places for offenses and for defensive protection against enemy attacks.

As they settled along the Aisne River, the German soldiers started to dig. They dug deep, and they dug long. They created intricate trenches that ran northwest and southeast for many miles. With their digging, the Germans were in the act of recreating the nature of the fighting on the Western Front.

French soldiers, bayonets fixed to their rifles, charge into no man's land during fierce fighting in northern France.
(ILN/Mary Evans Picture Library)

———

Over the last two weeks of September, when the French and British attacked the Germans at the Aisne, they were amazed to find the enemy soldiers dug into such sophisticated trenches.

The Allied attackers expected that the fighting would continue mainly above ground. But that period of battle had passed. From now on, almost everything on the Western Front would begin, and usually end, in the trenches.

Through the rest of 1914 into early 1915, while furious battles erupted all along the front in northern France and much of Belgium, the Germans expanded their trench system. The French, along with the British, whose troop numbers had increased in Europe by hundreds of thousands, responded with trenches of their own. Before the end of winter in 1915, the trenches on both sides, German and Allied, extended for 475 miles. They covered the distance from the Belgian coast on the North Sea to France's border with neutral Switzerland on the south.

In most areas, the opposing trenches were about five hundred yards apart. In a few places, the lines were so close that, on quiet nights, the soldiers on each side could make out conversations in the opposite trenches.

Each trench was protected in front by rows of tangled barbed wire. Behind the lead trenches, rows of three or four backup trenches took shape. Officers placed their headquarters in the rear trenches, which became sheltered hideouts where colonels and majors planned their attacks. Other back trenches served as communications centers. Soldiers waiting to go into action found temporary shelter in yet other trenches. Whole communities of fighting men lived underground for weeks on end during the battles on the Western Front.

As the Germans and Allies hunkered down, the generals on both sides realized that the war wouldn't end anytime soon.

Back in August, when the kaiser made a farewell speech to several of his troops, he said they'd be home before the autumn leaves fell. Britain and France thought they would halt the German attacks by Christmas. Everybody expected

This German trench on the Western Front may look deep, but other trenches were as much as thirty feet below ground. (ILN/Mary Evans Picture Library)

an early conclusion to the war. But now, dug into the trenches, the generals knew they had been wrong. The fighting on the Western Front had no foreseeable end. And it was going to be costly in lives lost.

In August 1914, France suffered 160,000 casualties. These were soldiers who were killed, wounded, taken prisoner, or missing. September claimed 200,000 more French casualties; 80,000 in October; 70,000 in November. The figures for December were more modest, about 40,000, only because cold weather shut down much of the fighting.

Though the French losses were the heaviest, soldiers from the other countries were also killed and maimed in frightening numbers. King Albert's Belgian Army lost 30,000 men to death on the 1914 battlefields. The figure for the British Army was roughly the same.

For Germany, whose total of soldiers killed in 1914 reached 240,000, the most disturbing deaths came during a battle that lasted through the late autumn near Ypres. The 25,000 dead soldiers weren't regular army veterans: they were young middle-class university students who had volunteered to fight.

The loss of the young students shook the kaiser. For the first time, he realized the price to be paid to show Germany's superiority to the rest of the world. The kaiser called the deaths at Ypres "the massacre of the innocents."

5 SUICIDE AND SURRENDER IN THE EAST

GENERAL ALEXANDER SAMSONOV FELT GRIPPED by despair. He commanded Russia's Second Army, and in mid-August of 1914, his superiors at Supreme Command in Moscow ordered him to lead his troops in an attack on the German Eighth Army, in Germany's most easterly province of East Prussia. But in anxious messages from the field, Samsonov begged for a delay.

He insisted that his soldiers needed a rest. The men were worn down from marching twelve hours a day, covering the vast distances through Russia's western regions toward the East Prussian border. A shortage of food added to the soldiers' troubles: they had been going whole days with only black tea for nourishment.

Brushing off Samsonov's objections, Supreme Command told him to take a run at the enemy without letting another day go by. Russia had promised to take pressure off the French on the Western Front by turning German attention to the east, and the Second Army must fulfil the promise. Samsonov understood his army's mission, but his confidence that the men could carry it out was shaky.

Russia's Czar Nicholas II reviews his troops in the late summer of 1914, before they head for battle against the Germans on the Eastern Front. His young son, Alexis, offers a salute of his own. (ILN/Mary Evans Picture Library)

————

A man of extreme emotions, Samsonov took pride in doing things the right way. At the Battle of Mukden in Russia's 1905 war against Japan, he thought his cavalry unit hadn't been properly supported by another unit under the command of an officer named Pavel Rennenkampf. The result was a sorry defeat.

Samsonov confronted Rennenkampf after losing the battle. When he didn't get the answers he wanted, Samsonov pulled back his fists and slugged Rennenkampf.

On August 24, 1914, reluctantly following orders, Samsonov led his men toward a showdown with the German Eighth. The Russian plan was to squeeze the Germans in a pincer movement – Samsonov's Second Army attacking from the south and the First Army simultaneously closing in from the north. Russia's First Army was commanded by none other than General Pavel Rennenkampf.

Russian soldiers set off on the long march to engage the Germans in battle hundreds of miles to the west. (ILN/Mary Evans Picture Library)

Samsonov knew that the Russians outnumbered the Germans. Together, his Second Army and Rennenkampf's First added up to nineteen divisions, more than double the nine German divisions. The big edge in manpower gave Samsonov comfort, though he may have wondered if he could rely on Rennenkampf's leadership in the battle ahead.

Early on the morning of August 25, German signalmen intercepted two internal Russian telegraph messages. The first came from Rennenkampf's headquarters, the other from Samsonov's. The messages revealed the details of the movements that both men planned in the coming days. One German officer was so excited when he read the intercepted communications that he wrote, "We have an ally! It is the enemy! We know all the enemy's plans!"

General Erich Ludendorff, chief of staff of the German Eighth, seized on this gift from the technical expertise of his signalmen. He had hurried from the Western Front to East Prussia only two days earlier. Ludendorff had been brilliant in his leadership at Liège and Charleroi. Based on those successes, Moltke chose Ludendorff to show the same bold spirit against the Russians.

The way Ludendorff read the intercepted messages, Rennenkampf's First Army was still too far away to bother the Germans for at least a couple of days. Meanwhile, Samsonov's Second, which was much closer to the Germans in distance, seemed not to have the faintest idea about the exact German location. Ludendorff ordered an immediate attack on the Russian Second Army.

Despite their weariness and hunger, Samsonov's soldiers gave a mighty effort in resisting the Germans. For three days in what was called the Battle of Tannenberg, taking the name from a nearby town, the armies fought back and forth until the weakened and outsmarted Russians began to crumble.

Rennenkampf's First Army never drew near enough to be part of the battle, and by the night of August 29, Samsonov had no choice but to retreat with his few remaining troops. Thirty thousand Russians were dead or missing. But even more alarming, the Germans had taken an astonishingly high number of Russian prisoners. Seventy-two thousand of Samsonov's soldiers gave in rather than fight on. Between death and surrender, the Second Army was just about wiped out at Tannenberg.

———

Like hundreds of thousands of other Austro-Hungarian soldiers, these men are only too glad to surrender to the Russians and get out of the war they hate. They are such contented prisoners that only one Russian soldier is needed to escort them to a prison camp. (ILN/Mary Evans Picture Library)

In retreat, in the midnight darkness of the twenty-ninth, Samsonov and his fellow officers hiked over soggy fields toward the Russian border seven miles away. With no moon shining in the sky and next to no light on the ground, the world seemed pitch-black. To make sure they didn't lose contact with one another, the officers held hands as they trudged through the countryside.

In utter despair, Samsonov spoke to the others about the shame that filled him. He held nothing against Rennenkampf, blaming only himself for the Tannenberg failure. "The czar trusted me," he said, talking of Nicholas II of Russia. "How can I face him after such a disaster?"

At one o'clock in the morning of August 30, the men stopped for a rest. In the deep gloom, Samsonov slipped away into a nearby wood. The next sound the junior officers heard was the firing of a pistol.

Samsonov had killed himself.

The defeat at Tannenberg revealed everything that was wrong with the Russian Army and its soldiers. Though the country's huge population meant Russia could send more troops into the field than any other nation, its men lagged far behind in their training and their dedication to the fight.

Eighty percent of the Russian Army was made up of peasants, the poorest of Russia's citizens. The peasant soldiers could neither read nor write. Understanding little about the world beyond their own villages, they never grasped why they were taken from their homes to fight the Germans, who lived far away in a country unknown to them.

When battles turned against the peasant soldiers, they often lost heart. To them, there was no great shame in handing themselves over to the enemy, especially when the peasants thought their czar and their generals had let them down. Surrender was better than death.

At Tannenberg, Samsonov and Rennenkampf made tactical blunders that cost Russian soldiers their lives. Their worst mistake was in allowing the Germans to fight the two Russian armies one at a time. Together, the armies stood a good chance of overwhelming the outnumbered Germans, but the failure of Samsonov and Rennenkampf to coordinate their attacks was fatal.

In early September, after the Germans took care of Samsonov's Second Army, they drove Rennenkampf's First Army back across the Russian border. The generals' failures in strategy – together with Germany's superior signals system – trumped the opportunity for victory.

Czar Nicholas II, in whose name General Samsonov committed suicide, didn't seem a monarch worth dying for. As a young man, Nicholas was given lessons in speaking English, in playing sports, and in basic military history. The limited education provided nothing close to the broad background he would need to command respect in his rule over the immense Russian Empire.

The czar took a passive attitude to events affecting his country, happy to let Russia drift as long as nothing got in the way of his own privileged life. In 1905, when Russian citizens revolted against the hard economic times, Nicholas allowed his Cossack military to shoot down the crowds of demonstrators. While other nations were putting democratic reforms in place, the czar saw no reason to permit such unimaginable changes in his country.

He was encouraged in his attitude by the czarina, Nicholas's sour and suspicious wife. The Russians knew her as Alexandra Feodorovna, but she was born Alix, the daughter of Princess Alice, the third child of Britain's Queen Victoria. The czarina's royal birth made her a first cousin to Germany's kaiser, a man she detested. The kaiser had a low opinion of both the czar and czarina. He said of Nicholas, "The czar is only fit to live in a country house and grow turnips."

Alexandra Feodorovna allowed few people into the royal inner circle. She made an exception in the case of a cunning monk named Grigori Rasputin, who claimed that a part of God was incarnated in himself. According to Rasputin, it was only through him that others could be saved in heaven. The czarina fell for Rasputin's message. She established him at court, making him one of the few outsiders to have her and her husband's ear.

Rasputin's presence in the czar's life was another sign of Nicholas's remoteness from his subjects. He was clearly a leader out of touch with his country, at a time when Russia's citizens were growing angry after centuries of rule by czars who took no notice of their struggles.

Field Marshal Franz Conrad von Hotzendorf of the Austro-Hungarian Empire may have been the most self-confident man in all of Europe. He believed he could handle any job his Empire asked of him in superb fashion.

In 1906, he was promoted to chief of staff of the Austro-Hungarian Army, inheriting a military that was sluggish and undersized. In his self-assured style, he rebuilt the army, and as Europe moved into the Great War, Hotzendorf had no doubt his army was the equal of any in Europe.

In the late summer of 1914, the Russians attacked the Austro-Hungarians in the Empire's northeast territory of Galicia. It was the first test for Hotzendorf's army, and he expected his men to blow the Russians away. In ferocious fighting, the Austro-Hungarians resisted mightily, but in the end, they were forced to fall back.

For all of the Russian Army's deep flaws, it still packed the punch to defeat Austria-Hungary.

The loss stunned Hotzendorf. But he recognized problems in his army that perhaps not even he could solve, problems created by the dramatic mix of twelve national groups, speaking nine languages, among the Austro-Hungarian soldiers.

About twenty-five percent of the men came from German ancestry; another fifteen percent were Hungarian. The Germans and the Hungarians fought magnificently for Hotzendorf. But he learned to expect nothing so wonderful from his army's Czech, Serbian, Slovak, and Croatian soldiers. These men made up forty-five percent of the army. Since they shared Slavic origins with the Russians, they saw no point in fighting and killing men who shared the same heritage.

During the battle at Galicia, the Slav soldiers made it clear that they placed blood before empire. Three hundred thousand of them surrendered to the Russians. Like the peasant soldiers at Tannenberg, the Slavs put up little firm resistance. They weren't unhappy to be taken prisoner, and their message to Hotzendorf was that Russia was not the natural enemy of Slavs like them.

Hotzendorf thought he could make up for the loss to the Russians by whipping Serbia, the Empire's most hated enemy. The Austro-Hungarians loathed the Serbs, but with Hotzendorf, the dislike grew into a full-blown obsession with the Serbs and Serbia. Between 1906 and 1913, he proposed a war against Serbia dozens of times, twenty-five proposals in 1913 alone.

The Austro-Hungarian emperor, Franz Josef, not wanting to stir more trouble among neighboring countries than necessary, turned down the proposal every time. But the Serbian assassination of Archduke Franz Ferdinand in 1914 changed everything. Not only was the archduke the heir to the throne, he was Hotzendorf's dear friend. In the summer of 1914, Hotzendorf at last received the go-ahead to invade Serbia.

Small and undeveloped, Serbia still had the potential to make things awkward for an invader. Geographically a mountainous country dotted with dense forests, it had few roads and no railroads. Its people were fighters who'd learned to handle weapons early in their lives.

When Serbia called its men to the army, everyone from boys in their early teens to elders in their seventies signed on. The regiments made up of the oldest fighters became affectionately known as "the uncles." Counting every soldier, teens to uncles, the Serbians put together an army of four hundred thousand, with hardly a weakness in the ranks.

On their way to battle the Austro-Hungarian invaders, the soldiers of Serbia include everyone from teenagers to men of "the uncles" regiment in their seventies. (ILN/Mary Evans Picture Library)

In late August of 1914, Hotzendorf made a full-fledged charge at Serbia, trusting his most formidable German and Hungarian units to wipe out the Serbs.

To Hotzendorf's embarrassment, none of his offense made a dent in the Serbian ranks. Out-manned and out-gunned, the stubborn Serbian Army knocked back the invaders. Hotzendorf regrouped and attacked again in December. The result was the same.

Hotzendorf was mortified at his failure, which was intensified by the complaints he received from Berlin. The kaiser fumed at the turn of events in the east.

From the beginning of the war, the German plan was for the Austro-Hungarians to handle the Serbs with ease in the southeast and to keep the Russian attackers in check in the northeast. If Hotzendorf and his army carried out their responsibilities, then Germany could concentrate on the more crucial fighting on the Western Front.

With the Austro-Hungarians turning out to be hopeless against both enemies, Germany needed to clean up the mess on the Eastern Front.

In the early winter, German units joined Hotzendorf's army in taking on the Russians. In monumental battles along fronts in the Carpathian Mountains of Austria-Hungary's northeast, the combined German and Empire armies came out as the clear winners. Though most of the troops in the fight were Austro-Hungarian, the success would never have come without Germany's soldiers and leadership.

When Italy entered the war on the Allied side in May 1915, it was the same story. The Italian Army soon engaged the Austro-Hungarians along the Isonzo River, in the mountains close to the Austrian frontier. In twelve separate battles of blood and intensity, Hotzendorf's army won the day, but only because Germany sent several divisions to bolster the Austro-Hungarian side.

It happened again in the autumn of 1915, when Hotzendorf once more invaded Serbia. On the third attempt at taming the Serbs, German troops and leadership produced a victory for the Austro-Hungarians. At last, Hotzendorf had reason to celebrate, though it took away from his pleasure to admit the debt to Germany.

By late 1915, Germany felt upbeat about its chances in the war. While the Schlieffen Plan hadn't made the impact that Germany counted on, there were other reasons for optimism.

Germany had rescued its partner, Austria-Hungary, from falling apart. The Germans had pushed the Russians back on their heels, though not out of commission. They were fighting the French and the British to a standoff in the trenches of the Western Front.

And, to the Germans' pleasant surprise, their one other comrade in the war – Turkey – had produced a success. The Germans expected little from the Turks. But against all odds, Turkey won a battle that the Allies would remember forever as a monumentally bungled opportunity.

6 GALLIPOLI

ENVER PASHA, TURKEY'S MINISTER OF WAR, was such a keen admirer of Germany that he wore his mustache with the ends clipped into upward tips, just like the kaiser's. Of all his country's new leaders, the "Young Turks" as they were called, Enver was the most passionate champion of an alliance with the Germans in the Great War.

Through the early months of 1914, other Young Turks disagreed with Enver, arguing in favor of joining the Allies. But it seemed doubtful that Allied countries would welcome the Turks as friends. To western leaders, Turkey was a nation that had gone into decline from its once-great glory. Winston Churchill, a British cabinet minister, spoke of "scandalous, crumbling, decrepit, penniless Turkey." *Who would want such a feeble country for a wartime partner?*

Russia had been a bitter enemy of the Turks for centuries, a situation that grew out of geography. Located at the eastern end of the Mediterranean Sea, Turkey controlled the Dardanelles and the Bosphorus. These were the two straits that gave Russia its only year-round trading route with the rest of the world. Since

Enver Pasha, Turkey's minister of war, argued that the Turks should join the Germans in the war against the Allies. (ILN/Mary Evans Picture Library)

Turkey did everything in its power to make Russia's passage through the straits as expensive and difficult as possible, the Great War presented a chance to the Russians to clamp down on the Turks. In one stroke, Russia could free up its trade route and give Turkey the punishment it deserved.

On August 2, 1914, the Turks signed a secret treaty with the Germans, giving Enver Pasha his way. The Germans appreciated Turkey, poor and downtrodden as the country seemed to be, because the Turks were in a perfect position to make trouble for Russia. Under the terms of the new treaty, Turkey and Germany guaranteed to support each other in a war with Russia.

The Turks didn't get into the shooting fight against the Allies until the first week of November, when Russia, England, and France formally declared war on Turkey. By that time, the Germans had helped Enver in whipping together an army prepared to take on all comers. Impatient to show off his new fighting force, Enver rushed to the head of 95,000 Turkish soldiers in an attack on the Russians in the Caucasus Mountains of southwest Russia.

In timing, strategy, and just about everything else, the action was the worst mistake of Enver Pasha's career. He attacked at the beginning of winter, when the temperatures in the mountains dropped far below zero and the snow came up to a man's waist.

Thirty thousand Turkish soldiers froze to death. Others died from starvation when their supply wagons couldn't push through the snowdrifts. Thousands more surrendered to the Russians just to get in out of the cold. In early January 1915, when Enver retreated back to Turkey, fewer than twenty thousand men from the original force were still alive and healthy enough to march away with him.

For the Russians, the fighting in the Caucasus Mountains counted as an easy victory. Still, the Turkish attack gave them second thoughts. They had enough to deal with in battling the Germans and the Austro-Hungarians. For the moment, the Russians decided that Turkey represented a problem they would rather confront in a year or two. In the meantime, Russia begged the Allies to ease the pressure by bringing their own actions against the Turks.

The British answered Russia's plea. In Britain's view, an attack on Turkey would not only aid Russia, it might possibly force Germany to fight on a third front. Such a battle could stretch German resources past the breaking point.

Gallipoli was a steep and rocky peninsula jutting out from the Turkish mainland. The Dardanelles strait ran along Gallipoli's southern shore, with the Aegean Sea on its north and west. In length, the Dardanelles stretched about thirty miles; in width, it varied from five miles at its widest to one mile at its most narrow.

Britain's initial plan was to send in a small naval force, instructing the ships to bombard the forts on the Dardanelles into submission. After such a pounding, Turkey would surely rethink its silly war against the Allies.

The young Winston Churchill was a leading advocate for an Allied attack on Turkey's Gallipoli peninsula. (ILN/Mary Evans Picture Library)

The idea of the naval attack came from Winston Churchill. Since he was the first lord of the admiralty, serving as the cabinet minister in charge of the navy, everybody in government assumed he knew what he was talking about. In mid-February of 1915, Britain ordered its Mediterranean fleet to proceed to the Dardanelles and fire away at the Turks.

The officer in the center of this rousing good cheer in the summer of 1915 is British General Ian Hamilton, who designed the Allied plan that was intended to capture Gallipoli. (ILN/Mary Evans Picture Library)

Eight British battleships and four French battleships cruised up the strait and blasted their guns into the Turkish placements. The Turks blasted right back, with equal power. That surprised the British. Britain's and France's battleships also ran into problems with the mines that the Turks laid in the middle of the strait. Nothing was proceeding the way Churchill anticipated.

The Dardanelles battle continued for a month, bringing added British ships into the fight. Turkish guns and sea mines sank two British battleships and one

French. More ships limped away, in need of repairs. The Turks were elated, their morale soaring from the depths it had fallen into after the ruinous fight in the Caucasus Mountains.

Soon Britain called off the Dardanelles naval attack, while Winston Churchill went back to his drawing board to think up another way of ridding the Allies of the troublesome Turks.

Churchill and the rest of the British cabinet decided next on an infantry invasion of Gallipoli. They dispatched one hundred thousand troops on a mission to conquer the Turks in a land battle on the peninsula.

As the leader of the new attack, they chose a sixty-one-year-old general named Sir Ian Hamilton. A poet and dedicated keeper of a detailed personal diary, Hamilton liked the solitary life. He was far from an inspirational military figure: not a cheerleader for his men, nor hands-on with his junior officers.

In putting together a strategy, Hamilton had no information about Gallipoli's defenses more up-to-date than 1906. He was working without adequate maps, and he could only guess at how many Turks might oppose the invading Allies. Nevertheless, Hamilton arrived at a scheme for attack in which he would concentrate his troop landings on Gallipoli's western coast.

The most veteran of the soldiers available to General Hamilton served in Britain's Twenty-Ninth Division. They were fighting men who had served in prewar colonial actions around the world. Hamilton assigned them to go ashore, guns blazing, on five different beaches at Cape Helles, on Gallipoli's southwesterly tip. A much smaller French force would attack at Kum Kale, a fort on the south side of the Dardanelles directly across from Cape Helles.

In what became the most controversial part of the attack, Hamilton chose raw recruits from Australia and New Zealand to land on a beach a few miles north of Cape Helles. Both Australia and New Zealand took their membership in the British Empire as a sacred duty. The two Dominions trained their young men in military tactics and in weaponry while they were still teenagers.

Whenever the Empire summoned them, the superpatriotic Anzacs (Australian and New Zealand Army Corps) would be ready to answer the call. Going into

The British warship Majestic, *on the right, is supporting the invading Australian and New Zealand troops at Gallipoli before an enemy torpedo sends it to the bottom of the Aegean Sea.* (ILN/Mary Evans Picture Library)

Gallipoli, the only credential these exuberant young soldiers lacked was war experience. None of them had ever fired a bullet in combat.

Just before sunrise on April 25, 1915, forty-eight troop transport ships carried the Anzacs from British battleships to the Gallipoli beach. Something seemed immediately wrong.

Perhaps by a mistake in navigation, perhaps through tricks in the sea currents, the transport ships put the soldiers onshore a mile from their designated landing place. The men found themselves on an undersized beach, surrounded on three sides by steep cliffs that came down to the water. It was the most discouraging of all landscapes for an invading force.

The only piece of good luck in coming ashore at such a remote spot was that few Turks waited in the area to oppose the Anzacs. The young men scrambled up the cliffs, climbing through the rocky ridges and deep ravines. It was an exhausting ascent, but the soldiers managed to reach several points as high as a mile and a half up the cliffs.

Late in the afternoon, a Turkish army commander named Mustapha Kemal spotted the Anzacs.

"To my mind," Kemal later wrote in his journal, "it was the vital moment of the campaign."

Australian and New Zealand soldiers row from transport ships to a Gallipoli beach. (ILN/Mary Evans Picture Library)

Kemal, a born leader, summoned his men to resist the invaders. The Turkish soldiers hesitated. They saw the thousands of Anzacs swarming up the cliffs toward them, and their instincts told them to run. But Kemal rallied the men. He harassed and coaxed and demanded. The Turkish soldiers responded: they turned and fought back, battling to hold their ground.

The Turks had the advantage of firing down on the enemy. They could pick off the attacking Anzacs as soon as they poked their heads into view. But when the Turks grew more confident and launched their own counterattacks, the stubborn Anzacs took their turn at cutting down the Turkish defenders.

The fighting raged for days. Halfway through the first week of May, the Turks had lost fourteen thousand men to death or wounds. The Anzac casualties totaled ten thousand. The Turks couldn't drive the Anzacs off the beach, nor could the Anzacs penetrate to the top of the cliffs. In military terms, the situation added up to a deadlock, which nobody was destined to win. Still, as the days stretched to weeks, neither side had the faintest thought of giving in.

This illustration dramatizes the dangers of a typical Australian attack on the Turks up Gallipoli's steep and rocky cliffs. (ILN/Mary Evans Picture Library)

Life under fire on the overcrowded Anzac beach turned brutal. The hot Mediterranean sun burned the men. Their diet, based largely on salty tinned beef, grew boring and unhealthy. Dysentery swept through the ranks, leaving the soldiers weak with fever. And the flies never went away: flies on the food, flies on men's bare skin, flies on every surface.

None of these hardships broke the Anzac spirit. The soldiers found relief in simple pleasures. They swam in the sea and tossed hand grenades into the water to kill fish, bringing a small upgrade to their menus.

———

The British attack at Cape Helles and the French attack at Kum Kale became just as stalled as the Anzac assault. In both places, the loss of men climbed to astronomic numbers, particularly in the bloodshed at Cape Helles. While the Turks couldn't knock the British off the cape, neither could the British fight their way past the defenders.

In early August 1915, Britain increased the Gallipoli force with seven more divisions to make a fresh start. Once again, the Anzacs surged forward on their beach. At the same time, the troops from the seven new divisions opened another front by charging ashore at Suvla Bay, a few miles to the north of the Anzacs.

For a few days, it looked like there was the chance of a British breakthrough at Suvla Bay. But the Turks brought in additional troops of their own and fought the British to another standstill. It was becoming clear to even the most optimistic of Britain's leaders that something had badly misfired in the Gallipoli strategy.

Back on the evening of April 25, the day of the first Anzac landing, Australian troops on the beach discovered a strange man in their midst. He wore civilian clothes and carried a notebook. A camera hung from his shoulder. The soldiers decided the man must be a spy, and they talked of executing him.

The stranger's name was Ellis Ashmead-Bartlett, and, as he proved to the soldiers, he wasn't a spy. He was a reporter for London's *Daily Telegraph,* the only journalist General Hamilton permitted on Gallipoli.

Ashmead-Bartlett had experience with combat conditions. He fought as a lieutenant with the Bedfordshire Regiment in the Boer War, and he covered the Russia-Japan War of 1905 in his newspaperman's role. Ashmead-Bartlett stayed on Gallipoli for months. Based on his battle background, he developed a negative view of Britain's handling of the entire campaign. He called it "a ghastly and costly fiasco." He thought that Hamilton was an out-of-touch leader. The general rarely set foot on Gallipoli's shores, preferring to direct the attacks from aboard a ship in the Aegean. Ashmead-Bartlett's point was that Hamilton's distance from the fighting led to breakdowns in communication with his commanders in the field.

Since British officers censored Ashmead-Bartlett's reports before he telegraphed them to London, he could mention few of the criticisms. But in early September, an Australian journalist named Keith Murdoch presented Ashmead-Bartlett with a chance to get his uncensored story to England.

Murdoch was traveling from Australia to Britain, where he would report on the war for two of his home country's newspapers. He interrupted his long journey in order to visit the Anzac beach for a few days. While Murdoch was on Gallipoli, Ashmead-Bartlett gave him a letter in which the English reporter blew the whistle on Hamilton's failures in conducting the campaign. Murdoch's job was to deliver the letter to British Prime Minister Herbert Asquith.

Before Murdoch reached England, British Army agents tracked him down and took away Ashmead-Bartlett's letter. Disappointed that he had failed in his mission, Murdoch decided to write his own letter. He drew on his brief Gallipoli experience, together with Ashmead-Bartlett's more thorough observations, to put on paper an eight-thousand-word cry from the heart.

Murdoch condemned the leadership of Hamilton and the other British generals. He wrote that these men's "conceit, self-complacency and incapacity" resulted in what he called the "murder" of Australia's finest young men. The Anzacs were losing their lives to British incompetence, and Murdoch said he and his countrymen shouldn't take it any longer.

Murdoch got his letter into Asquith's hands. He delivered other copies to Australian Prime Minister Andrew Fisher and to the press of both countries. The letter caused an instant sensation.

The British government already recognized that things were a mess in Gallipoli. With Murdoch's letter appearing in the newspapers, the public in Britain and the Anzac countries got in on the secret. Everybody, particularly Australians and New Zealanders, made their anger known.

The British cabinet scrambled to clean up the scandal. Hamilton was the first to go: the cabinet fired him. For good measure, more British generals were kicked out of their Gallipoli posts.

Before the Australian and New Zealand troops withdraw from Gallipoli, they bid farewell to their fallen comrades. (ILN/Mary Evans Picture Library)

To replace Hamilton, the cabinet appointed a general who was a dozen years younger, a man with a solid record on the Western Front. His name was Charles Monro, and he needed only a short time in Gallipoli to realize he must wind down the hopeless battle. The cost of Gallipoli had grown too steep, and the end appeared nowhere in sight. More than 250,000 Allied soldiers were dead, wounded, or missing. Even more Turks, about 300,000 of them, met the same fate.

Under Monro's direction, the Allies' withdrawal moved briskly ahead. By the second week in January 1916, not a single British soldier remained on Cape Helles, not a single Australian nor New Zealander on the Anzac beach.

Australians came to look on Gallipoli as the event that defined their country. They said that the soldiers left for the war as representatives from the six states that made up their country and returned as members of one nation.

April 25, the day of the landing at Gallipoli, has become the most valued of Australia's national holidays. Every year on this date, Australians gather for sunrise services to honor Gallipoli and the men who fought and died there, in the act of creating modern Australia.

7 AT SEA

WHEN THE MOMENT ARRIVED FOR ADMIRAL John Jellicoe to accept his appointment as the British navy's commander in chief, he turned unexpectedly reluctant.

For two decades, Jellicoe's superiors had been grooming him to lead Britain's Grand Fleet of hundreds of warships. A small intense man, Jellicoe was by nature exceedingly polite and deferential to his seniors. As he rose up the levels of command, he looked forward to his final promotion. But when the day came to step into the top position, Jellicoe thought the timing was wrong.

It was late July of 1914. War with Germany lay right around the corner. In Winston Churchill's post as first lord of the admiralty, he instructed Jellicoe to hurry north from London to Scapa Flow, the port in the Orkney Islands off the Scottish mainland where the Grand Fleet tied up. Jellicoe's orders from Churchill

The man with the imposing profile is Admiral John Jellicoe. In May 1916, he commanded Britain's navy against the Germans at the Battle of Jutland, the most colossal warfare in naval history. (City of Toronto Archives, Fonds 1244, Item 9758)

were to tell Admiral George Callaghan, the resident commander in chief, that he was out of a job and that Jellicoe was taking over.

Nobody doubted that the navy needed Jellicoe in command. More than any British officer, he understood how to deploy ships equipped with the biggest naval guns. The guns were the offensive force that would decide the inevitable battle against the German navy.

But Jellicoe sent a telegram to Churchill from Scapa Flow, saying it would be "embarrassing and painful" to relieve Callaghan of his command at the moment in naval history that would present the older admiral with the most thrilling opportunity of his career. Churchill wouldn't listen.

Jellicoe blitzed Churchill with more telegrams, begging him to keep Callaghan in place. Churchill refused.

At 8:30 on the morning of August 8, Jellicoe gathered his nerve to break the bad news to Callaghan. The moment was as excruciating as Jellicoe feared. Callaghan was heartbroken, but he cleared out his quarters to make room for the new commander. By assuming command, Jellicoe felt he had committed a terrible act of betrayal to Callaghan.

On that August day in 1914, the Grand Fleet was destined to go into the biggest sea battle in history. But the question arose whether Jellicoe was tough enough for the fight. Even Churchill had doubt.

"Jellicoe," he said, "is the only man on either side who could lose the war in an afternoon."

On the first day of the war, the British navy dispatched a ship called the *Telconia* on a delicate assignment. The *Telconia*'s usual work was to lay and maintain the undersea cables that carried Britain's international telegraph messages. On August 5, the ship was ordered to slip into the waters off the German port of Emden on the North Sea and cut Germany's own undersea cables.

With slick skill, the *Telconia* succeeded in the cutting operation. From then on, Germany could no longer send messages by way of its cables. Now it had to rely on cables controlled by Sweden and the United States. But the Germans knew that Britain had no difficulties in picking off the German messages from either of the two foreign cables.

To get around its serious new communications problem, Germany wasted no time in developing a series of codes. For the rest of the war, all German messages, particularly those to and from its warships, were delivered in secret codes.

In London, the British navy assembled a unit devoted to figuring out the German codes. The men who served in the unit, cryptologists as they came to be called, were civilians. Because nobody had training in the largely unexplored area of cryptology, the new employees came from varied backgrounds. Some were skilled in mathematics; others brought fluency in German to the unit. A few were simply academics who could focus on any complex subject with ferocious concentration.

All of these people, creating their trailblazing science on the fly, worked in Room 40 of London's Old Admiralty Building. Though they soon outgrew the poky little room, the cryptology unit was thereafter known as Room 40.

Early in the war, Room 40 came into a piece of amazing good luck. On August 14, the Russians sank a German cruiser named the *Magdeburg* in the shallow waters of the eastern Baltic Sea. The *Magdeburg* carried three signal books, each of them containing details of the new German codes.

As the ship went down, the *Magdeburg*'s captain managed to burn one signal book and toss the other two, weighted with lead, into the Baltic. Since the water wasn't deep in the area, Russian divers had no trouble scooping up the two signal books from the floor of the sea.

Two weeks later, the Russian naval attaché in London offered the signal books to Winston Churchill. The instant Churchill laid eyes on the documents, he recognized their value. He delivered the books to Room 40, where the cryptologists went to work in detecting the principles behind the codes.

Within a few months, Room 40 broke the German codes, giving Britain the means to intercept every German signal. Aided by two more lucky recoveries of other German code books, the cryptologists discovered clues to decoding virtually all the messages that the Germans fired off to their ships around the world. Even better, Germany never realized that its codes were being deciphered.

But all was not perfect with Room 40's remarkable accomplishment. The naval officers who served as the cryptologists' bosses couldn't quite bring themselves to accept Room 40. The code-breakers were mere civilians, not men who shared in the brotherhood of the Royal Navy. Many officers refused to take them seriously, hesitating to believe the word of the strange Room 40 men who said they had cracked the German codes.

On the night of November 1, 1914, before Room 40 had completed its code-breaking, five German warships under the command of Admiral Maximilian von Spee lurked in the Pacific Ocean, close to the Chilean port of Coronel. The German ships, far from home, were part of Germany's early plan to hunt down

A British battleship fires a mighty salvo at German ships during the Battle of Jutland. (ILN/Mary Evans Picture Library)

Allied ships in all parts of the world. The British navy had similar ideas about attacking German ships. Two of Britain's cruisers in the Pacific, the *Monmouth* and the *Good Hope,* had stopped in Coronel for refuelling. When the cruisers pulled out of the port, Spee's warships opened fire.

Having no idea that the Germans were so close, the British were unprepared for the attack. In the darkness, the Germans sank both the *Monmouth* and the *Good Hope,* taking the lives of more than fifteen hundred sailors. The short battle represented the first British defeat at sea in one hundred years. Losing the two ships at Coronel haunted Britain's navy for the rest of the war.

Encouraged by the sensational success at Coronel, small fleets of German ships roamed the world's seas in the following months, making trouble everywhere they went. The Germans attacked Allied ships in the South Pacific and in the Atlantic. They hounded transport ships carrying Anzac troops from Australia to the war in Europe. For several months, the quick-striking German ships seemed invincible.

Then Admiral Spee's attacks grew more daring. In early December 1914, Spee and his five ships took on a squadron of British battle cruisers near the Falkland Islands, in the South Atlantic. This time, the overconfident Spee picked a fight with a tougher, faster, more heavily armed opponent. The British battle cruisers blew four of Germany's five ships out of the water, and Admiral Spee himself went down with his flagship, the *Scharnhorst.*

Of the five German ships, only the *Dresden* escaped from the Falklands battle, fleeing east across the Atlantic. Four months later, British ships cornered the *Dresden* off the Cape of Good Hope, at the foot of Africa. When the British sent the *Dresden* to the bottom of the ocean, the German navy took the defeat as a warning to cut back on its worldwide marauding.

Inspiring as the British found their victories against the *Dresden* and the rest of Spee's ships, they knew that the Royal Navy couldn't reclaim their rule of the seas until they showed their superiority over the entire German fleet.

———

Through 1914 and 1915, Britain's Grand Fleet lay at anchor in Scapa Flow, at the top of Scotland. Germany's High Seas Fleet was stationed further south and to the east, in German ports on the North Sea between Holland and Denmark. Ships from the two massive fleets met in occasional small skirmishes up and down the North Sea. But no head-to-head battle involving both fleets at complete strength took place.

The problem that faced Germany's navy was that the only route to international waters beyond Britain was through the North Sea. But the British fleet maintained a large squadron of ships on constant patrol across the North Sea waters, between Scotland and Norway. If Germany wanted to get clear of the North Sea and attack the Allies in other areas of the world, it needed to break through the blockade enforced by the British patrol ships. For most of two years, the Germans risked nothing, and its fleet remained in port.

When Admiral Reinhard von Scheer took command of the German navy in January 1916, he brought a fresh attitude to his country's sea warfare.

An aggressive leader, Scheer argued to the kaiser that the time had come to set loose Germany's High Seas Fleet in all its power. Admittedly, it wasn't as large as Britain's Grand Fleet, but Scheer thought he could make up for this difference with his fleet's skills in naval weaponry. He insisted that it was wrong to let the navy rust in uselessness while Germany's armies were engaged in a life-and-death struggle all over Europe.

Agreeing with Scheer, the kaiser approved a new offensive naval strategy.

In late May 1916, Scheer made plans for a major naval breakthrough. His idea was to lay a trap for Britain's North Sea patrol. The scheme called for a comparatively small fleet under Admiral Franz von Hipper to lure the patrol into a chase. Scheer and the full High Seas Fleet would take up position further south, lying in wait for the unsuspecting patrol ships as they pursued Hipper. The British would make an easy target for Scheer. He'd blast the patrol to pieces before it recovered from the shock of falling into the trap. Scheer had no notion at this stage of engaging the full Grand Fleet in battle. He was satisfied to take Britain's patrol squadron out of operation and free up German passage through the North Sea.

On the evening of May 30, 1916, Room 40 decoded intercepted German signals originating with Admiral Scheer. The signals revealed that Scheer and his High Seas Fleet would be pulling out of port early the next day.

That night, as soon as Admiral Jellicoe got the Room 40 report of Scheer's intentions, he got the full Grand Fleet ready to leave Scapa Flow. By 10:00 p.m., he and the fleet were at sea. Already steaming through the North Sea, well ahead of Jellicoe, was the regular British patrol fleet under the command of Admiral David Beatty.

A few hours later, at one o'clock on the morning of May 31, Franz von Hipper set to sea with the German fleet that was to lead Beatty's patrol ships into the

Admiral Jellicoe's warships, enemy shells splashing into the sea around them, steam into the fight against the German fleet. (ILN/Mary Evans Picture Library)

trap. An hour and a half after Hipper's departure, Scheer led his High Seas Fleet into the southern end of the North Sea.

In the early morning hours, Room 40 decoded German messages confirming that Scheer was now at sea. But that wasn't the way Rear Admiral Thomas Jackson interpreted Room 40's information. Jackson, who was in charge of the Royal Navy's flow of communications, was one of the doubters of Room 40's value. Perhaps as a result of his bias against the cryptologists, he got the idea from the intercept that Scheer's fleet was still in port.

Jackson passed on the incorrect version to Jellicoe. Led to believe that Scheer wasn't yet under way, Jellicoe took his time in traveling south. With the Germans unlikely to clear port for a few hours, Jellicoe thought he could be deliberate in his approach to the battle ahead.

But the misinformation represented a possible lost opportunity for Jellicoe. If Jackson hadn't sent it, Jellicoe's ships might have sped up and caught the High Seas Fleet completely off guard. An early success could have been Britain's.

By noon of May 31, the Grand Fleet and the High Seas Fleet were steaming in the general direction of each other. Scheer had no idea that Jellicoe had set off from Scapa Flow, and Jellicoe was uncertain of Scheer's precise location. Still, on May 31, almost 250 ships were pointed toward a sea fight that became known as the Battle of Jutland. The name was taken from the nearby Danish peninsula: Jutland would be the most colossal battle in naval history.

About two-thirty on the afternoon of May 31, as Beatty's fleet charged south, one of its smaller ships, a destroyer named the *Petard,* sighted an advance destroyer from Hipper's fleet. The *Petard* fired at the German ship. Though the shell flew wide, it was the first shot in the Battle of Jutland.

Beatty accelerated his southern run. Six battleships made up his primary strength. Battleships were the largest and most powerful ships in any fleet. Almost fifty ships of smaller sizes – destroyers, cruisers, mine-laying ships, even a submarine or two – supported the six Beatty battleships.

More than an hour passed before Beatty came upon the full Hipper fleet, which was made up of slightly fewer ships. Still, with five battleships, Hipper almost matched Beatty in that crucial category.

At the Battle of Jutland, the dashing Admiral David Beatty shows an independent streak that annoys his superior, Admiral John Jellicoe (ILN/Mary Evans Picture Library)

At three-thirty, Beatty met Hipper in the first of the day's pitched battles.

The British battleships blasted away at Hipper's fleet. Hipper's battleships returned the fire. As the fight continued, the German guns inflicted more damage than the British. Hipper scored hits on two of Beatty's cruisers: the *Queen Mary* and the *Indefatigable*. The blows were far more than just glancing. Both ships blew up. As the rest of Beatty's fleet watched in agony, the *Queen Mary* and the *Indefatigable* sank to the bottom of the sea.

Thrilled with his success, Hipper turned his ships and raced further south. He would have liked to spend more time fighting Beatty, sinking British ships, and showing his strength to the enemy patrol. He felt he could get the best of Beatty, but fighting the British patrol ships wasn't his job: he was assigned to lead Beatty into Scheer's trap. And that was what he intended to do.

Hipper's ships continued south, firing as they went. Beatty, his guns still blazing, followed not far behind, having no suspicion that he was steaming toward a German trap.

To Hipper, the German plan was working just as Scheer had calculated. Beatty stayed on Hipper's tail as Hipper grew closer and closer to the waiting High Seas Fleet. The Germans were certain that a tremendous naval victory lay just ahead.

Then, just when Hipper and his officers were beginning to congratulate themselves on their cleverness, Beatty got lucky. The alert lookouts on Beatty's lead ships, studying the sea ahead through their binoculars, caught sight of the High Seas Fleet. The lookouts warned Beatty that Scheer's ships loomed on the horizon, just beyond Hipper. If the sighting had come even minutes later, Beatty would never have been able to avoid an attack by Scheer. Now aware of the danger, he thought he had just enough time to swing out of the path of the oncoming battleships.

Beatty shouted the orders to turn around his fleet. Reversing course was a slow process for such big vessels. But gradually, with one eye on Scheer's fleet growing larger in view just to the south, Beatty got his ships pointed north. He accelerated and went on the run, having two motivations for flight. The first was to save his ships from certain annihilation at the hands of Scheer's far more powerful fleet. The other was to lead Scheer into a battle against Jellicoe's Grand Fleet.

Scheer took after Beatty. The whole point of his trapping scheme was to eliminate the British patrol that confined him to port. Sheer had no intention of pulling the plug on his plan.

As Jellicoe churned south through the late afternoon, he felt uneasy. He hadn't yet made up the time he lost because of Admiral Jackson's misinterpretation of the Room 40 intercept. The weather was another problem. During the afternoon, shifting mists covered the sea and limited Jellicoe's view over the water.

Jellicoe worried that he hadn't heard from Beatty. Throughout the fight with Hipper and brief encounter with Scheer, Beatty sent no word to Jellicoe. He held off on contacting Jellicoe for so long that Jellicoe's first hint of Beatty's location came close to six o'clock, when he heard the thunder of gunfire through the mists up ahead.

"What I wish," Jellicoe said to the officers on his battleship, *Iron Duke,* "is for someone to tell me who is firing and what they're firing at."

Within a few minutes, Jellicoe got his answers. He and his Grand Fleet came upon ships that he recognized as Sheer's High Seas Fleet, which was firing at the fleeing Beatty. Jellicoe, reacting to the opportunity that presented itself so suddenly, aimed his fleet at Scheer. He was ready to go to battle against the mighty German navy.

When he looked up ahead, Scheer was astonished to discover Jellicoe's fleet bearing down on him. The German intention all along was never to take on the entire Grand Fleet; he wanted only to cripple Beatty's patrol ships. But now Scheer realized he had no choice: the showdown with the British was unavoidable. He wouldn't back down.

The Grand Fleet had twenty-four battleships and more than eighty smaller ships. Scheer, however, had just sixteen battleships. But Scheer, never short of confidence, believed his ships could still come out ahead in a fight with the Grand Fleet.

While the German gunners showed skill and a go-for-broke spirit, their guns thundered at Jellicoe. They scored two consecutive direct hits on the British cruiser *Invincible.* The hits detonated *Invincible's* store of shells belowdecks. When the shells blew up, *Invincible* split in half. Both halves sank abruptly, taking most of the sailors aboard, and the ship's commander, Admiral Sir Horace Hood, went down with his men.

The loss of Hood and *Invincible* shook Jellicoe, but he knew his superior numbers gave him an advantage. His guns blasted at the German ships. The two fleets, circling around each other, fired round after round of shells. Ships on both sides took fatal hits, sinking to the bottom of the sea. It was hard to keep track of the losses in the middle of battle, but both sides sensed that the Grand Fleet was suffering more sinkings than the High Seas Fleet. Still, after three-quarters of an hour of fighting, it was Scheer, growing wary of Jellicoe's larger fleet and its relentless pounding, who turned away in a hasty retreat to the south.

With Scheer gone over the horizon, Jellicoe took stock of his fleet's condition, counting his losses and considering his next action. He had barely begun the stocktaking operation when something entirely unexpected made him change direction.

In the distance to the south, Jellicoe could see the High Seas Fleet heading toward the British ships. The German retreat had lasted no more than thirty minutes before Scheer decided to return to battle. He had lined up his sixteen battleships in single file, his support ships around and behind them. It was in a long vertical line that Scheer was to meet the British in a battle that he anticipated would be a final German triumph. As confident as ever, he drove his fleet full speed ahead at the Grand Fleet.

This was the moment that Jellicoe's lifetime of naval training had prepared him for. This was going to be the encounter at sea that Winston Churchill had chosen him to fight. Churchill knew Jellicoe as the man who understood the deployment of ships and guns in naval strategy better than anyone. Jellicoe's expertise with armaments was the reason Churchill named him commander in chief. Now was the moment when Jellicoe needed to show his worth as a naval leader. And, as Scheer's fleet charged over the sea, bristling for battle, Jellicoe had to make his all-important decisions in a hurry.

Steadily, firmly, Jellicoe gave his orders without hesitation. He based his strategy on the deployment of his twenty-four battleships, directing that they line up in a formation called line abreast. It meant that the twenty-four ships positioned themselves side by side by side, all of them in a straight line stretching for seven miles.

On board the British battleships, the commanders were adroit in following Jellicoe's instructions. No ship faltered and no ship broke formation. Jellicoe's horizontal line of ships was running at Scheer's vertical line. Navy men referred to the deployment as "crossing the T." As Jellicoe knew, the alignment meant that his battleships had clear shots up and down the line of Scheer's battleships. Scheer had no such easy targets. Jellicoe based his chances for success on this difference.

As the two fleets closed within shooting distance of each other, the Grand Fleet wasted no time in ripping shell after shell at the High Seas Fleet. Their fire was unrelenting. Having the advantage in the number of targets they could fix on, the British exploited the advantage for all it was worth.

Scheer's ships were thrown off balance by the British horizontal alignment. They blasted their guns at the enemy battleships, but their shots were flying wide. They couldn't draw clear targets on the British, and their guns had no hope of matching the bombardment from the Grand Fleet. The fighting lasted just ten minutes, but in that short space of time, the Germans managed a mere two hits on the British ships. The British guns outscored the German guns by an overwhelming margin, landing twenty-seven hits on the High Seas Fleet.

Jellicoe's deployment had proven to be a stroke of naval genius, and Scheer, having no answer, turned his ships once again to the south. This time, conceding the battle, he raced full steam for Germany.

The victorious Jellicoe had the option of chasing Scheer and perhaps landing a final disabling assault on the German fleet. But he turned away from the scene of the battle, just as Scheer had done. Possibly Jellicoe feared torpedoes from the smaller German ships that were still in the area. He chose caution over risk.

All of a sudden, Jellicoe changed his mind: he reversed his fleet to take after Scheer. But he was too late. The German battleships were already ten miles away and out of Jellicoe's reach. He ended the pursuit not long after he began it.

Through the night of May 31 and into the morning of June 1, the smaller ships from the two fleets continued to fire at one another. Both sides suffered severe hits, but the main bout in the Battle of Jutland had ended.

Scheer lost six ships at Jutland, none of them battleships. Jellicoe's losses in the day's battles added up to fifteen ships, a number that likewise included no battleships. On Scheer's side, 2,532 sailors died in the fighting compared to 6,092 of Jellicoe's sailors. On the basis of this, the kaiser declared a victory for the High Seas Fleet.

It was a view shared by many British people, government and public. The British had been expecting a smashing victory. They'd counted on another Trafalgar. Trafalgar had been the most resounding of all British naval triumphs, when Admiral Lord Horatio Nelson's fleet defeated the French and Spanish navies off Spain's Cape Trafalgar on October 21, 1805. But, in the general British opinion, Jutland had been no Trafalgar, and Jellicoe had been no Nelson.

In Britain, Jutland was regarded as a disappointment and probably a defeat. Jellicoe was the man who took the blame. His critics accused him of lacking the toughness for the job of polishing off the German fleet. When he had a chance to finish the Germans once and for all, after Scheer's ships took twenty-seven hits, he turned away until he ran out of time. Too many Britons refused to forgive him.

Photographed in Toronto's harbor in 1917, this German U-boat is captured when it strays too close to Canada's Atlantic coast. (City of Toronto Archives, Fonds 1244, Item 745)

——

In November 1916, Jellicoe was relieved of his command. He received an appointment as first sea lord, a title that put him in overall charge of the Royal Navy. But his duties kept him at a desk, not at sea. The more freewheeling Admiral David Beatty became commander in chief.

On Christmas Eve 1917, Jellicoe lost his post as first sea lord. A year later, he was sent on a tour of Britain's Dominions, advising the Empire's navies on their reorganization. It was not much more than a public relations job.

As events unfolded in the war's final year, it at last became clear that British popular opinion about Jutland was terribly wrong: Jellicoe hadn't lost the great sea battle. The result was far more positive than Jellicoe's critics had insisted. It was much closer to the truth to say that Jellicoe had won at Jutland.

German ships were so damaged by the hits from Jellicoe's gunners that the High Seas Fleet never again became a factor in the war. German warships ventured out of port for a handful of small battles, but the full fleet avoided the North Sea except for one harmless run to Norway and back.

The battered German navy stayed in port, which was just where the British wanted it. Unopposed, the Grand Fleet continued its blockade of Europe.

In the end, much of the opinion about Admiral John Jellicoe was reversed, and the reluctant commander in chief emerged at last as the hero of Jutland.

8 ARTHUR CURRIE'S MILITARY MIND

I N THE YEARS JUST BEFORE THE WAR, Arthur Currie's real estate agency in Victoria, BC, was close to broke. As a way of meeting potential new clients and saving his business, Currie joined the 50th Regiment of the Gordon Highlanders, the local militia unit. On weekends, the Highlanders would get together to march, study military tactics, and play war games.

A chubby man, without the physical presence usually expected of a leader, Currie had a natural gift for the military. He understood intuitively the strategies of moving around large groups of fighting men, even if it was only in practice battles. His talents won him rapid promotion up the Highlanders' ranks. Soon he became the unit's colonel and commander in chief.

Currie's position at the head of Victoria's militia did nothing to help his real estate agency, which went out of business in 1914, leaving him deep in debt. But with the outbreak of war, the regular Canadian Army had other things in mind for

General Arthur Currie of Canada wins a solid reputation as a top Allied strategist on the Western Front. (Toronto Reference Library)

Currie. Recognizing his military gifts, the army made him a wartime officer and sent him to Europe.

At the Battle of Ypres in the spring of 1915, Currie commanded the Second Canadian Brigade, fighting as part of the British contingent. The Germans, who held the small Belgian city, launched an attack against the French and British in the surrounding countryside. For the first time in the war, Germany fired poison gas on the Allied soldiers, suffocating and disabling thousands of them. Forced back by the gas and by the fury of the German assault, the Allies retreated about two miles. But Currie's Second Canadian Brigade put up the stiffest Allied resistance, stalling the German advance in their sector.

This Canadian soldier, fighting in France, doesn't forget the girl he left behind. (City of Toronto Archives, Fonds 1244, Item 829)

The battle lasted from April 22 to May 25. Although six thousand Canadians were killed, wounded, or taken prisoner at Ypres, Currie showed the qualities of a first-rate combat commander. He put much care into his battle plans, paid attention to detail, and made the extra effort to keep his casualty rate low.

Even in the first year of the war, Allied soldiers thought their commanders often sent them into hopeless slaughters. The complaining grew louder as the war continued and troops died by the hundreds of thousands, but no soldier was ever heard to criticize Arthur Currie's treatment of the men he commanded. He took it as a personal responsibility to protect the lives of his soldiers.

None of Currie's abilities were lost on his British superiors. It was unheard of for a man who wasn't a career army officer to get an appointment to a major wartime post in the field. But in plain, blunt, sensible Arthur Currie, the British saw the exception: he was a rare civilian who deserved promotion to tough leadership jobs.

In the year after Ypres, Currie was mostly caught up in administrative duties, organizing and training Canadian troops. But in the last two years of the war, he emerged as one of the most effective military leaders among the Allies. Currie was so capable and organized that David Lloyd George, the British prime minister from December 1916 to 1922, praised him as the best of the British and Empire generals. Lloyd George let it be known that, if only Currie were British and not a colonial, Lloyd George would have named him to the command of the entire British Expeditionary Force.

Throughout 1916, in the time before Vimy Ridge, the Germans and the Allies on the Western Front took turns bringing brutal offenses against one another.

Germany went first. On February 21, German troops attacked the French position at Verdun. Germany's generals didn't look on Verdun as an essential target. Protected by a series of forts, the small French city stood on a high point of land above the Meuse River, about forty miles west of the German border. In the overall German war plan, capturing Verdun was a challenge, not a necessity.

In the first couple of days of the fighting, German troops drove the French into retreat. They appeared to be on schedule to capture the city. A French general named Noël de Castelnau, General Joffre's deputy, rushed from Paris to Verdun to make a judgment about the military situation. Castelnau decided that the battle over the city should be a number one priority for the French. It was a test of the country's ability to defend itself, and France must resist Germany at Verdun with all its vigor. As soon as the Germans recognized that the French were taking an aggressive attitude in defense of the city, they stepped up the strength of their attack.

For the next five months, both sides poured men, guns, and shells into the Battle of Verdun as if they had a never-ending supply of all three. German and French cannons and howitzers fired more than twenty millions shells. Villages vanished under the onslaught; forests were obliterated, the landscape forever changed. Two hundred thousand men on each side were killed or wounded.

When the fighting began to wind down in early July, the exhausted Germans had overrun a few miles of French countryside, but they hadn't captured Verdun. The battle might have been considered a victory for France, but it was hard to convince French soldiers who had seen such death and destruction that they were on the winning side.

Later in 1916, General Douglas Haig brought big dreams to the Battle of the Somme. Haig was the commander in chief of the British Expeditionary Force. As a military man, he was both highly political and deeply religious. He ingratiated himself with Britain's royalty, making a close friend of King George V. The royal connections did no harm to his army career. In battle, Haig thought he was invincible because, in his belief system, it was God's divine plan for him to lead the British to victory, beginning at the Somme.

The earth under the gently rolling country beside the Somme River was dry and chalky, making it perfect for easy digging. When the Germans occupied the area in the autumn of 1914, they built trenches thirty feet deep. Nests of machine gunners guarded the trenches from every angle. And barbed wire was stacked so densely in front of the trenches that it was hard to imagine any attack penetrating it. For almost two years, realizing how complex the Germans had made their defenses, the Allies steered clear of the Somme.

General Douglas Haig enjoys the pomp and fancy costumes that go with his command. (Toronto Reference Library)

In 1916, Haig took a new attitude. He intended for the Somme to become the scene of what he called the big push. Assembling an army of almost eight hundred thousand men, ninety percent of them British, Haig was convinced he could break through the German lines. He thought a victory at the Somme would be the first of many in the toppling of Germany's armies up and down the Western Front.

On June 24, the British artillery opened a bombardment on Germany's Somme position. It lasted virtually around the clock for a week. The British aimed their heavy guns at burying the Germans in their trenches, while the smaller guns were to tear apart the rows of enemy barbed wire.

The bombardment ended on June 30, and at 7:30 the next morning, British infantrymen climbed out of their trenches and into the attack. July 1 was bright and sunny, a gorgeous summer day. Most of the British soldiers were young volunteers experiencing their first taste of combat. They felt cheered and confident, as if they were off on a lark. In some battalions, these innocents kicked footballs out in front of the lines as they trotted into no man's land.

On the first day of the Battle of the Somme, the young men soon discovered that nothing worked as Haig planned. Britain's heavy guns had done no damage to the German troops, who were sheltered in the thirty-foot-deep trenches. The smaller guns hadn't cut the barbed wire, but only made it more tangled. And the German machine gunners, safe and sound, lay in wait to mow down the British troops as they advanced onto the fields.

German bullets caught many soldiers before they took a step away from the British trenches. Far more died outside the barbed wire, unable to get past the tangles and helpless to find cover in the open spaces. Machine-gun fire tore the British to pieces. Of the one hundred thousand soldiers who attacked the Germans that day, twenty thousand were killed. Forty thousand suffered wounds. The losses could have been worse, but the German soldiers, amazed at the enemy's courage and stupefied by the slaughter, let up on their fire when the British survivors turned back to their own lines.

Haig sent more young troops to attack the next morning and on many mornings after that. The fighting continued for months. Britain's men gave as good as they got, charging at the Germans, returning fire for fire. But they produced no great results. In a very few areas, the British penetrated as deep as seven miles into the German position. But in other sections of the Somme, the battle lines never advanced by a single yard from the beginning of the fight.

The Battle of the Somme ended on November 18. The Germans lost six hundred thousand men to death and wounds. The combined losses of the British and the French, who fought in the southern Somme region, added up to about the same number.

In December 1916, the British made plans for another major attack on the Western Front. The new action would take place the following spring in the neighborhood

Canadian soldiers set up their machine guns in shell holes on the fields leading to Vimy Ridge, just over the horizon on the top right. (ILN/Mary Evans Picture Library)

of a town called Vimy, which lay about forty miles north of the Somme. An elevated ridge of land ran just to the west of Vimy. The ridge was nine miles long, with a commanding view of the surrounding countryside. On the ridge's east side, railway lines leading into the town of Vimy stretched all the way to Germany.

The Germans had captured Vimy Ridge early in the war and held on to it. They brought in more soldiers and supplies on the busy railroad, becoming so dominant in the area that they easily knocked back every British and French attack on their valuable position.

For the new attack on Vimy, Canadian troops would take the major role, fighting under the overall command of a spit-and-polish British general named Sir Julian Byng. A total of one hundred thousand Canadian soldiers would go into the fight divided into four divisions, each commanded by a Canadian officer. Arthur Currie would lead the First Division. Currie's methodical approach to military problems had caught Byng's eye. In preparing for Vimy, he assigned Currie the task of putting together a report on the failures at the Somme to determine what went wrong and how Byng could avoid the same mistakes at Vimy.

Currie had some personal experience at the Somme, having fought with the Canadian battalions during the last weeks of the battle. To build on his knowledge, Currie interviewed several of the senior British officers who had survived. He made extensive notes and wrote out everything he learned on dozens of sheets of foolscap. By a happy coincidence, the French happened to invite Currie to visit Verdun in early January. He used the opportunity to grill French officers about their experiences in the terrible battle of the previous spring and summer. Thorough and relentless, Currie wanted to know everything about Verdun and everything about the Somme. "He pumped us all dry," one British officer said.

When Currie presented his report to Byng later in January, his main message was about preparation. If Byng and his officers thought they knew how to prepare their men for battle, they were in for a surprise. Currie's ideas took preparation to an entirely new level.

Currie wanted every man who went into battle at Vimy to know his particular job in absolute detail. It wasn't just the officers who must understand the battle plan; it was every soldier from private to general. And they needed to know other people's jobs as well. If a corporal was killed or wounded in battle, then the private who replaced the corporal had to be up to speed on his new duties. Currie ordered forty thousand maps of the area around Vimy, detailing the location of German defenses and the points of the Canadian attack. Every soldier was ordered to memorize the maps.

Byng agreed with Currie's ideas, but there were many more still to come. The Canadians rehearsed the upcoming battle through February and early March as Currie suggested, learning their parts the way a company of actors would master their roles in a Shakespearean play. From hundreds of photographs of the German lines that pilots in Britain's Royal Flying Corps took from the air, Currie and his fellow officers put together a replica of the Vimy battle area. All the positions were marked out with thick white tape on empty fields deep behind the Allied lines. Under the officers' direction, the soldiers were taken through their assignments for battle day. Each man learned where he was supposed to go in no man's land, what his responsibilities were, and which German defenses he needed to attack.

The Canadians laid twenty miles of railway tracks to carry men and supplies safely from the rear into their trenches. They built three miles of plank roads and repaired twenty-five miles of local roads. To make sure there would be no break-down in communications during the fighting, they buried twenty-one miles of cable and strung sixty-six miles of cable above ground.

Currie's personal motto during the war was NEGLECT NOTHING. In getting ready for Vimy, he and the rest of the Canadians didn't leave anything to chance. They dug secret underground tunnels reaching from their trenches to points far into the fields near the German positions. When the time for battle arrived, Canadian soldiers would spring out of the ground much closer to the German lines than the enemy could ever have imagined.

The men dug a second set of longer and narrower tunnels that ran all the way to the first line of German trenches. In the tunnels below the Germans, the Canadians set massive mines in place, just waiting to be detonated.

———

These Canadian infantrymen, who have just driven the Germans from Vimy Ridge, look down on their final objective, the town of Vimy. (Canadian War Museum AN-19920085)

The Canadians' preattack artillery bombardment opened on March 20. Paying particular attention to the German barbed wire, the gunners put a valuable new device into play: a 106 fuse, which was designed to set off a high-explosive shell on contact with the wire – not above or below it, but squarely on the wire. The fuse guaranteed that the wire would be shredded.

In the first week of the preattack bombardment, following the procedure mapped out by Currie and the other officers, just half the artillery fired, dumping 140,000 shells on the Germans. In the second week, the rest of the guns and howitzers took over, concentrating their fire on German supply lines. The purpose was to keep the enemy from bringing shells and other ammunition up to their trenches. So effective was the artillery's work in the second week that the Germans called it "the week of suffering."

———

At 5:30 on the morning of April 9, Easter Monday, a day of snow and sleet, the Canadian infantrymen fixed their bayonets. The attack along the miles of front was about to begin.

Each of the four Canadian divisions was responsible for a section of the front, varying in width from a mile to almost three miles. Currie's First Division had the most southerly section, the one with the longest stretch of land to cover. From the First's starting line to the Farbus Wood, a forest at the foot of the ridge, was more than four thousand yards.

Within the area, the Germans were set up in two heavily fortified positions, running across no man's land and up the ridge. The First's objective was to crush both defenses and all the other German obstacles in their path.

Precisely at 5:30, the guns behind Currie's First Division trenches rained shells on the Germans for three minutes. At the same time, gunners detonated two of the massive bombs under the German trenches. Then machine guns swept the fields for four hundred yards up ahead. When the machine guns fell silent, the men of the First attacked. Some came up and out of their trenches while others sprang from the tunnels dug into no man's land.

Moving with speed and discipline, knowing their roles from the days of rehearsal, the Canadians were on top of the first enemy lines before the Germans had time to react. German soldiers expected an attack from the Canadians, but not so soon. The barrage of shells and the underground bombs had confused them.

Shortly before seven that morning, the First Division overran the first German line. They killed hundreds of enemy soldiers and made prisoners of hundreds more.

The Canadians paused while their artillery fired another barrage at the second German line. When the barrage lifted, the next wave of soldiers advanced toward the German defensive line. The men picked their way around shell holes and bomb craters, threw hand grenades at the German machine-gun nests, and took prisoners of the overwhelmed enemy soldiers who saw no choice but to give up.

———

At noon, following another barrage from their big guns, the First's infantry blasted through the second German line of defense and reached Farbus Wood. They found several German artillerymen dead, killed in the barrage. The rest of the gunners had fled, abandoning their heavy weaponry. Never before in fighting on the Western Front had the Allies advanced so fast that they captured German artillery.

The Canadians of the First surged up the ridge's western slope. Their advance proceeded like clockwork. The Germans, knowing they stood no chance against the fast and efficient assault, went on the run to the east. Before nightfall, the First's section of Vimy Ridge's crest belonged to the Canadians.

The attacks of the Second and Third divisions made equally smooth progress that day, across no man's land and up to the top of the ridge. Only the Fourth Division, responsible for the most northerly section of the attack, ran into trouble. Their area included the ridge's second most imposing peak, almost seventy-five yards high. The peak was called the Pimple, and the Germans, reinforced with fresh troops, defended it with such determination that the Fourth needed three more days of fighting before they captured the Pimple.

In midafternoon of April 12, all of Vimy Ridge was in Canadian hands. The victory didn't come without a cost. Casualties for the four divisions added up to more than ten thousand men. Over thirty-five hundred were deaths.

No British army had made a deeper advance into German territory in the two and a half years of the war than the Canadians at Vimy. It was a victory that surprised and pleased the British and French, who hadn't succeeded when they tried to capture the ridge. They looked at the Canadians with new respect.

Canada's leader in the victory was Arthur Currie, the failed real estate agent from Victoria. Currie may not have been a whiz in the realty business, but he showed inspiration as a leader of men in wartime. After the triumph at Vimy, Currie got his reward when he received a promotion to lieutenant general. A few weeks later, Canadian soldiers were given their own recognition with the creation of the Canadian Corps. Led by Currie as their commander in chief, the Canadians were now a unit on their own.

From then on, having proved themselves at Vimy, Canada's soldiers would follow the overall strategic direction of the British, but they would fight as an independent force in all the battles still ahead on the Western Front.

9 DISORDER IN THE RANKS

SIEGFRIED SASSOON SEEMED AN UNLIKELY British war hero. Even his name had the wrong ring. His mother, from a family of well-known English sculptors, named him Siegfried after the opera by her favorite composer, Richard Wagner. Wagner happened to have been German.

It was Siegfried's father, a Jewish businessman, who made the Sassoon family fortune. With an allowance from the senior Sassoon, young Siegfried spent the years before the war following his pleasures. He hunted wild game. He played cricket. He wrote poetry. Then Germany invaded Belgium, and Siegfried gave up his charmed life.

To his family's astonishment, Siegfried joined the army on the first day of the war. He rose to the rank of second lieutenant in the Royal Welsh Fusiliers. In battles on the Western Front, he was such a daring leader that his men nicknamed him Mad Jack.

As a British army officer, Siegfried Sassoon fought bravely on the Western Front, but he is best known for his poetry condemning the war. (Toronto Reference Library)

During one engagement against the Germans at Brest, France, in June 1916, Lieutenant Sassoon needed to courageously guide his soldiers through a fierce German counterattack. The action that day won him the Military Cross for valor on the battlefield.

In the summer of 1917, wounded in another battle and convalescing in England, Sassoon turned against the war. He was fed up with the killing and thought Britain should negotiate a peace treaty with Germany. But he felt convinced that powerful British munitions manufacturers who profited from the war wouldn't allow the fighting to stop anytime soon. Sassoon wrote about his views in a five-paragraph statement. He called it his declaration.

"I have seen and endured the suffering of the troops," he wrote, "and I can no longer be a party to prolonging these sufferings for ends which I believe to be evil and unjust."

London's most influential newspaper, the *Times*, published the declaration. A member of parliament read it aloud in the House of Commons. Since Sassoon was a famous war hero, the declaration attracted criticism of the government all over Britain.

Embarrassed by Sassoon's words, the army announced that he was suffering from neurasthenia. Better known as shell shock, neurasthenia was a mental disorder brought on by the horrors of the battlefield. The army shipped Sassoon to Craiglockhart Military Hospital in Scotland, where he would be out of public sight.

Craiglockhart specialized in treating officers for shell shock. Nightmares and hallucinations tormented the hospital's patients. They developed stammers in their speech, and their bodies jerked with twitches they couldn't control. The war had driven some poor souls close to madness.

While nightmares plagued Sassoon, he wasn't nearly as troubled as most patients at Craiglockhart. In no time, he was getting out of the hospital for rounds of golf. He found plenty of opportunity to write poetry. The poems, which later earned Sassoon his reputation as a distinguished writer, made passionate antiwar statements. But no amount of therapy at Craiglockhart cured Sassoon of his hatred for the war.

In November 1917, Sassoon arrived at what seemed a contradictory decision. He said he was going back to the Western Front.

Though he hadn't changed his feelings about the war, he saw a greater duty in returning to his men. They needed leaders who put the soldiers' lives first. In Sassoon's mind, nobody at home cared enough about the ordinary British men in the trenches. Sassoon cared: he would do his best to keep his own men alive.

Six months after his return to the fighting in France, on July 18, 1918, in a battle near a town named Saint-Floris, a German bullet creased Sassoon's head. The wound wasn't severe enough to threaten his life, but it brought an end to Sassoon's days on the battlefield. He'd done everything in his power to protect the soldiers he commanded.

While Sassoon's story attracted attention and entered into the history books, it wasn't unique. Many more Allied officers and soldiers came to hate the war as much as Sassoon. All through the ranks of the armies in Britain, France, and Russia, men feared and resisted battle. They would do almost anything to avoid the blood and death of the war they were ordered to fight.

On August 15, 1917, Sergeant Bill Alexander of the First Canadian Infantry Division quit the war.

Alexander was born in poverty in England in 1880. Orphaned at eleven, he got by on his own until he turned seventeen and joined the King's Royal Rifles. He served in the army for eight years, though never in combat.

After his discharge in 1905, Alexander immigrated to Canada. He found a good job as manager of an automobile tire business in Calgary. But as soon as war broke out in 1914, he enlisted in the 10th Battalion of the Royal Canadian Infantry Corps. With his past military service, he soon was promoted to sergeant.

Overseas, Sergeant Alexander's unit fought in countless battles on the Western Front, losing hundreds of men to death and wounds. Altogether, Alexander was on the firing lines for thirty-three months. He missed action in a couple of battles: once when he was ill in hospital and again while he recovered from an inflamed knee. Otherwise, he carried on as just another soldier doing his duty.

On August 15, 1917, the 10th Battalion drew the assignment of attacking Hill 70, a strategically important German position. Sergeant Alexander's job was to lead a platoon of men in D Company. But on the morning of the fifteenth, at zero hour for the attack, Alexander was nowhere to be found. A corporal took over the leadership of Alexander's platoon, conducting the men into a day of fighting that cost the Canadians more than four hundred casualties.

Two days later, Alexander turned up in the nearby village of Les Brebis. He told his superior officers that he missed the Battle for Hill 70 because a stray German shell had knocked him down. Then he changed his story, claiming he had fallen sick. But he hadn't reported the illness to his commanders in the field. Nor did he show any signs of lingering health problems.

Alexander's superiors ordered him arrested and held for court-martial. The charge was desertion. Five weeks later, on September 17, Alexander appeared at the court-martial, presided over by three officers.

In a hearing lasting a day, the prosecution put in evidence that Alexander, an experienced soldier, had failed to report for duty at the time of an important battle. His absence left the much-less-experienced corporal to lead Alexander's men. The officers judged this a serious offense, risking the lives of soldiers who took orders from the inexperienced corporal. They convicted Alexander of desertion.

As penalty, the court-martial gave Alexander the most severe sentence: death by firing squad.

On the evening of October 17, 1917, Canon Frederick Scott learned that Alexander, a man Scott hadn't yet met, was to be executed the following morning. Canon Scott served as the Anglican padre to the First Canadian Infantry Division for the entire war. As much as any soldier, he understood the horrors of the battlefield. On the night of the seventeenth, the padre spent two hours with Alexander in his jail cell, offering comfort and religious guidance.

As the two men talked, Scott became moved by Alexander's predicament. Alexander had fought for almost three years and had seen hundreds of his comrades killed in battle. Wasn't it possible that his nerves had snapped on August 15, that the war had stretched him beyond his ability to handle one more day of shooting and killing? Could Alexander have suffered shell shock? Scott decided that he would attempt to save Alexander's life.

In the next hours, driving through the rainy night on muddy back roads, the padre called on senior officers who had the authority to commute Alexander's sentence. Along the way, Scott learned that only a small percentage of men convicted of desertion were sentenced to the firing squad. Almost all received terms in prison instead. But a few deserters needed to be executed as a lesson to other soldiers who might think of leaving their posts during battle.

Speeding along the back roads on his mission to rescue Alexander, Canon Scott didn't hesitate to wake up colonels and generals, begging them for help. All the officers told Scott that they sympathized with him, but that he was too late to appeal. Alexander, they said, was a soldier who must die for his desertion.

Just before sunrise, Scott drove to the place where Alexander's execution was to be held. It was an empty field near a small hill, a couple of miles behind the Allied trenches.

Officers led Alexander, blindfolded, before a firing squad of ten soldiers picked at random from the Canadian infantry. One of the rifles issued to the firing squad held blank bullets, meaning that no soldier could be certain his own rifle was a killing weapon. On the signal from an officer, the ten rifles fired at Alexander. He fell to the ground.

"I have seen many ghastly sights in the war," Canon Scott later wrote, "but none of them brought home to me so deeply the hideous nature of war as that lonely death on the misty hillside in the early morning."

In the course of the war, Canada executed twenty-five of its soldiers. Britain and all but one of the nations of the British Empire believed in the firing squad as an answer to problems of troop discipline. Australia was the exception, the only

Private Stephen Fowles of Winnipeg, Manitoba, served on the Western Front in Canada's 107th Infantry Battalion. In the spring of 1918, a court-martial convicts him of desertion, and he is shot to death by a firing squad. (A. B. Godefroy)

member of the Empire that doubted the wisdom of punishing military offenders with death.

The total numbers of soldiers ordered to the firing squad by Britain and the rest of the Empire countries, including Canada, reached 348 by the war's end. The large majority of these men were convicted of desertion, but some were found guilty of such other offenses as cowardice, disobedience, and mutiny.

At the end of April 1917, the soldiers of France began to talk of mutiny.

Earlier in the month, on April 16 – a day of rain, sleet, and snow – the French were ordered to try for a breakthrough in the German lines at a town near the Aisne River called Chemin des Dames. The attack, which lasted a week, was a failure. It produced no breakthrough, and the cost in men added up to 130,000 casualties. Twenty-three thousand of them were deaths.

French soldiers had already died in the war on a staggering scale. More than 300,000 died in 1914; 334,000 in 1915; 217,000 in 1916; and about 100,000 in the first four months of 1917. Many of the French troops felt that the loss of life at Chemin des Dames was just too much to bear, after all the killing that had gone before. The thought of mutiny began to circulate among the soldiers.

By June, almost half of the French soldiers on the Western Front were refusing to fight. Hundreds of thousands said they wouldn't return to the trenches. They told their officers that they were on strike: they had entered a state of mutiny.

The leaders among the mutineers spoke in terms that Siegfried Sassoon would have recognized. They demanded peace negotiations with the Germans. To them, only French munitions-makers and other businessmen were benefiting from the war. Everybody else suffered while the profiteers grew rich.

Though the leaders talked this way, the ordinary soldiers went on strike for far more modest reasons. They wanted better food, and they wanted more leave from the front lines. The soldiers needed time to return home, where they could help the parents, wives, and children they had left behind.

Conditions for French citizens on the home front had grown increasingly grim with each year of the war. Food was in short supply. Prices were skyrocketing. People had to work twice as hard just to scrape by. The unhappy French civilians supported the troops in their mutiny. The combined pressure from both soldiers and civilians convinced the French government to treat the striking troops with tact and sincerity.

———

The officer with the confident stride in the center is French General Henri-Philippe Pétain, who handles the crisis when France's soldiers mutiny against the war in 1917. On the left, in flowing black, is General Joseph Joffre, the heroic leader in France's early battles. (ILN/Mary Evans Picture Library)

A general named Henri-Philippe Pétain, popular among the soldiers, had been appointed commander in chief of the French Army in the early spring of 1917. It was up to Pétain to settle the mutiny before he got on with the rest of the war.

Pétain had commanded France's defense a year earlier, at the battle for Verdun. Though two hundred thousand French soldiers died or were wounded in the fighting, the men looked on Pétain as a soldier's soldier. They thought he would treat them fairly in the mutiny.

Pétain had no intention of going easy on the mutiny's leaders. He ordered 3,427 courts-martial. Five hundred and fifty-four soldiers received the death penalty, though only forty-nine of them were actually put in front of firing squads. The rest had their death sentences commuted to terms in prison.

Pétain showed generosity in handling the great mass of the ordinary troops. He improved the quality of the soldiers' meals, and he introduced a program of rest and retraining. Since the retraining took place far behind the lines, Pétain's program was a way of letting the men know that there would be no more battles for the immediate future. The soldiers had time to return home.

From June 1917 to July 1918, during the mutiny, the French made no attacks on the Germans along France's two-thirds of the Western Front. Enough men took defensive duty in the French trenches to handle possible German action, and the French artillerymen were ready to let fly if they were needed. But for thirteen months, France didn't dare to launch a single significant offensive.

The most incredible part of this strange interlude was that the Germans never noticed how quiet it had become on the French sections of the Western Front. If the German generals had registered the lack of activity, they might have brought an attack that would surely have flattened their enemy. But nothing like that happened.

The German Army had other things on its mind. Britain's strategy was always to be far more active than the French in raiding and shelling enemy positions. The British continued to keep the Germans busy along their one-third of the front during the months of French inactivity.

Germany's leaders had additional distractions. Russia in the east was one, and the Italians on the Austrian-Italian border were another. If the French seemed to the Germans to be subdued, then the Germans were glad to find themselves temporarily freed from one more concern on the battlefield.

Under Pétain's patient guidance, the French mutiny wound toward its end. By July 1918, the soldiers had returned in full strength to the battle lines. They hardly rejoiced in the prospect of more fighting. Élan had practically vanished as one of their qualities, but the soldiers were ready to do their duty. For the entire length of the Western Front, it was once again war as usual.

In the winter of 1916–1917, Russia's peasant soldiers were as miserable as the French. They ate poorly and often not at all. They had no leave. And they heard nothing except bad news from their families back home.

These Russian soldiers aren't running into combat with the Germans. They are abandoning the war, like hundreds of thousands of their comrades, in the early autumn of 1917. (ILN/Mary Evans Picture Library)

But what made the Russian situation different was the Russian soldiers' attitude. Unlike the French, who appreciated the need to resist the Germans, the Russian peasant soldiers saw no purpose to the war. It was futile and pointless, a war not worth fighting.

At home, Russia's transportation and supply systems had broken down. Food and fuel weren't reaching the cities. People were going hungry, and the czar's bumbling government had no ability to straighten out the mess.

In February 1917, the citizens began to protest the food shortages by flocking into the streets of Petrograd, Russia's capital city. "Bread!" the people chanted. The demonstrations continued for days, and on February 25, the freakishly warm winter day brought out an enormous crowd of two hundred thousand screaming protestors. They went on a rampage through Petrograd, taking out their fury on everything in their path, wrecking shops, and battling the police.

Czar Nicholas, as disengaged as ever from Russia's people, relied once again on his Cossacks. Supported by the army, the Cossacks were to put down the mob in the streets. But this time, the czar and the Cossacks got a surprise. This time, the soldiers took the people's side: they turned against the czar and drove away his Cossacks. The army was in the process of bringing down the government.

Two months earlier, in December 1916, the czar had lost his spiritual advisor, the cunning monk Grigori Rasputin. Much of the Russian elite felt disgust at Rasputin's influence over the royal family. On December 17, a handful of nobles invited Rasputin to supper and slipped cyanide into his wine. When the poisonous cyanide didn't work, one of the hosts pulled out a gun and shot Rasputin dead.

The people and institutions that propped up the czar – Rasputin, the army – were falling away. A revolt swept through the country, and the bewildered czar suddenly had nowhere to turn. General Mikhail Alexeyev, chief of staff of Russia's army, warned Nicholas that the unrest at home would have disastrous effects on the war against Germany.

"It is impossible to ask the army calmly to wage war," Alexeyev wrote to the czar, "while a revolution is in progress in the rear."

On March 2, Nicholas gave up his throne. Russia no longer had a czar, and no monarch succeeded Nicholas. Russian socialists, who were in the process of taking power, imprisoned the czar, the czarina, their son, and four daughters in a house in Tobolsk, a distant town. In a matter of days, Russia's last royal family went from palace luxury to humble confinement.

———

Russia's Czar Nicholas II is looking even more melancholy than usual in this June 1917 photo. He has abdicated his throne and is living in the humble custody of the new Russian government's armed guards. (ILN/Mary Evans Picture Library)

Shortly after the czar's abdication, a socialist politician named Alexander Kerensky emerged as the leader of Russia's Provisional Government. Kerensky implored the army to get on with the fight against the Germans.

While Russia's peasant soldiers had affection for Kerensky, the warm feelings didn't translate into new enthusiasm for the war. After one halfhearted offensive against the Austro-Hungarians in June, the army went into necessary retreat. Kerensky could do nothing to rally the troops.

In the autumn of 1917, the more radical Bolsheviks under Vladimir Lenin seized power from Kerensky. Lenin had no interest in continuing the war, wanting to concentrate on his social revolution inside Russia. After brief negotiations with the Germans in October, Lenin signed an armistice that was intended to last for three months.

Russia's soldiers took advantage of the lull in fighting to remove themselves from the war. By surrender and desertion, they got what they had wanted from the very beginning of the Battle of Tannenberg in 1914: they broke free of the war they didn't understand.

When Vladimir Lenin's Bolsheviks seize power in Russia in 1917, Lenin's first order of business is to get his country out of the war. (Toronto Reference Library)

The peasant troops surrendered to the enemy in such numbers that, by the end of 1917, Germany and the Austro-Hungarian Empire held four million Russian soldiers as prisoners. Many more Russians deserted and walked back home.

"The men," Lenin said, "voted for peace with their feet."

In February 1918, Lenin agreed to a treaty on strict terms set by Germany. The Germans required the Russians to hand over 450,000 square miles of the country's western territories. The land made up a vast area equal to three times the size of Germany itself. One quarter of Russia's population lived in the territories, which accounted for a third of the country's agricultural production.

Despite the treaty's burden, Lenin signed. He needed peace, not the distraction of war, while he got on with the business of his social revolution.

On July 16, 1918, Bolshevik agents called on the czar and his family at the house where they were being held. The agents led the family down to the cellar. One of them shot the czar in the head. After a pause, the others fired a fusillade of bullets at the czarina, the son, and the four daughters. None of the royal family survived.

10 UP IN THE AIR

Billy Bishop had a bright idea. A twenty-three-year-old Canadian fighter pilot, Bishop was already an ace flyer with Britain's Royal Flying Corps. By the end of May 1917, he had shot down twenty-two German planes. All of his victories took place in battles thousands of feet in the air over Allied and German territory on the Western Front.

But in early June of that year, it occurred to Bishop to try something completely different. He thought he might catch the Germans off guard if he attacked their planes early in the day, before they got off the ground.

Bishop set his alarm for three o'clock on the morning of June 2. Waking up groggy but eager, he pulled on a flying suit and gulped a cup of hot tea. A mechanic wheeled Bishop's silver Nieuport plane out of the hangar at Filescamp Farm, the British air base fifteen miles behind the Allied lines in northern France. Bishop jumped into the cockpit and took off in the early darkness.

At first light, around four-thirty, after losing his way in the gloom, he arrived over the German aerodrome near Cambrai, deep behind enemy lines. He dropped

Giant German zeppelins, flying by night, drop their loads of bombs on London and other British targets, creating a reign of terror that lasts almost two years. (ILN/Mary Evans Picture Library)

his altitude, leveling off the Nieuport at six hundred feet above the ground. As he swooped across the airfield at a speed close to one hundred miles per hour, Bishop spotted a line of Albatros fighter planes preparing for a day's action.

German machine gunners down below became alert to the sight and sound of the Nieuport. They opened fire. Bishop flew through the hail of bullets that peppered his plane and blasted his own machine gun at an Albatros that had just become airborne. Bishop, almost scraping the ground, was no more than 150 feet from the enemy plane. The Albatros took the full force of Bishop's fifteen rounds of ammunition: it tipped and crashed to earth.

As Bishop continued his low sweep, another Albatros caught his eye. The German plane was just beginning to gain altitude. Bishop fired from three hundred feet. The bullets went wide, but the sudden attack rattled the Albatros's pilot so badly that he slammed into a tree. Bishop had a fraction of a second to get off another blast. His aim was perfect. The Albatros disintegrated.

Behind the controls of a fighter plane, no pilot in Britain's Royal Flying Corps tops the records of Canadian ace Billy Bishop. (ILN/Mary Evans Picture Library)

Bishop then pulled back on his plane's control stick, heading straight upwards. A third Albatros came at him. Both planes fired. Both missed. The two pilots jockeyed for better shooting positions.

Easier to maneuver than the Albatros, Bishop's Nieuport swung beneath and slightly behind the German plane. Bishop opened up his gun. His bullets struck the Albatros's fuselage just in front of the pilot. The plane's engine died, and the Albatros plunged nose-down into the ground.

Bishop turned west for home. He had forty miles to cover before he reached the safety of Filescamp Farm. He knew word would have gone out to other German air bases to hunt down the Nieuport that had done so much damage at the Cambrai aerodrome.

Bishop needed to hurry. He unhooked his overheated machine gun and dumped it overboard. That got rid of one hundred pounds of weight and gave his plane extra speed.

A few miles further on, he caught sight of four German fighter planes two thousand feet above him, flying in the same direction. The odds were against Bishop: four armed enemy planes versus his unarmed Nieuport.

But the Germans hadn't seen Bishop. He held his position, two thousand feet directly under the German planes. He turned when they turned, changed altitude when they changed, copied their moves, and stayed at an angle that made it difficult for the Germans to spot him. The tactic worked. Bishop kept the four German planes oblivious to his presence below them.

When the moment came for him to dive down and away from the Germans, Bishop got into an even tighter spot. The dive took him low over the German battle lines on the ground. Antiaircraft guns sent shrapnel whizzing at Bishop's plane, and one of the Nieuport's wings was shredded in the assault. Bishop struggled to keep the plane in the air.

"I flew in a daze," Bishop said later. "For the only time in my life, I thought I was losing my senses."

He kept enough of his wits about him to coax the Nieuport to Filescamp Farm. With bullet holes in the fuselage and one wing effectively useless, Bishop still coasted safely across the British field. The time was five-thirty, just a couple of hours after he had taken off. While Bishop's fellow pilots slept in their beds, he had shot down three German fighter planes.

Two months later, on August 10, Bishop received the Victoria Cross for his heroic work.

The war of 1914 to 1918 was the first when men fought in the air as well as on land and sea. Though the air battles were not nearly as decisive to the war's outcome as the land battles, or even as sea fights like the Battle of Jutland, the contest for supremacy in the sky introduced influential new concepts in fighting to modern warfare. From the outbreak, Germany plotted to force the Allies into surrender with attacks on Britain by motorized air balloons of a colossal size. Called zeppelins after the German who invented them, the pilot-operated

The millions of pieces of metal and debris scattered across the ground are the remains of a zeppelin shot out of the sky by a Royal Flying Corps plane. (ILN/Mary Evans Picture Library)

airships cruised at sixty miles per hour, had a range of four thousand miles, and could carry loads of up to sixty bombs.

Beginning in early 1915 and continuing for almost two years, zeppelins terrorized the south of England. The ships crept across the English Channel in the dead of night. From out of the dark skies, they unloaded their bombs on London and other cities. Zeppelin raids killed more than four hundred civilians, wounded thousands more, and caused untold damage in destroyed homes and buildings.

Frightening as the physical damage was, the zeppelins had a deeper effect on British morale. A zeppelin could hover in place for twenty minutes while the pilot picked out targets. The eerie sound of the ship's motors, bringing with it the prospect of bombs, unnerved the people down below who lived in constant fear of the zeppelin attacks.

British antiaircraft guns failed at bringing the airships down largely because the ships were kept at heights of ten thousand feet or more, beyond accurate antiaircraft range. Fighter planes were just as helpless. Their bullets seemed incapable of effectively penetrating the tough rubberized cotton that covered each zeppelin's aluminum framework. The zeppelins grew so disdainful of the opposition that a fleet of no less than fourteen airships made a deadly attack on British targets on the night of September 2, 1916.

The very next night, September 3, a Royal Flying Corps pilot named William Leefe-Robinson took his fighter plane high in the sky on zeppelin patrol. Robinson's machine gun carried powerfully explosive ammunition mixed with tracer bullets.

At two o'clock in the morning, over the Thames River, Leefe-Robinson sighted a zeppelin headed in the direction of London. He raked the zeppelin with three drums of his explosive ammunition, firing at the huge airship from every angle until he had no more bullets left.

To Leefe-Robinson's amazement, the zeppelin exploded in flames. The powerful ammunition, combined with Leefe-Robinson's accuracy, had done the job. He watched from his fighter plane as the zeppelin blew into a million pieces that fluttered to earth.

Minutes before the Royal Flying Corps observer gets stuck in the tree, he is studying German positions on the Western Front from an air balloon tied to the ground and floating eight thousand feet in the sky over British lines. When a German fighter plane fires at the balloon, the observer bails out with his parachute, falling safely to Earth until the tree gets in the way. (ILN/Mary Evans Picture Library)

It was the beginning of the end for the zeppelins' reign of terror. The airships continued their raids in the following months, but British fighter planes, inspired by Leefe-Robinson's success, kept up the resistance that he had started. To the relief of the British public, the German zeppelin threat soon vanished.

Almost all fighter pilots, men like Leefe-Robinson and Billy Bishop, knew nothing about flying until they got into the war. Roland Garros of the French air force was an exception. Taking up aviation in 1909, he became so skilled that, in 1913, he

The puffs of white smoke are exploding shrapnel from German antiaircraft fire. They are directed at the British biplane on an observer mission over enemy lines in northern France. (ILN/Mary Evans Picture Library)

was the first man to fly solo across the Mediterranean Sea, from Fréjus in the south of France to Tunisia in North Africa.

In March of 1915, Garros put his aviator's mind to the problem of fitting a machine gun to his fighter plane. Every airman agreed that a machine gun placed directly in front of the pilot's cockpit gave the best chance for firing accurately at an enemy plane. The trouble was, the machine gun was just as likely to shoot off the attacking plane's own propeller, sending plane and pilot into a tailspin.

Garros thought the best answer lay in a deflector device. He made one by hammering heavy metal plates around his plane's propeller blades. The plates, Garros figured, would deflect bullets away from the propeller, allowing other bullets to fire between the blades and strike enemy planes.

On April 1, Garros took his Morane-Saulnier fighter plane with its deflector blades into the sky for the first time. A German plane came Garros's way. He aimed at it and pressed the trigger on his machine gun.

The plane is an early Fokker, the first German warplane designed so that the machine gun, placed in front of the cockpit, fires through the propeller's blades. (ILN/Mary Evans Picture Library)

Bullets flew out of the gun, ricocheting off the deflector plates in all directions. But several bullets zipped between the propeller blades and hit Garros's target. Smoke burst from the German plane, which tipped downwards into a spiraling crash.

France celebrated Garros as a national hero. Up until then, few Allied pilots had success at bringing down German planes by machine-gun fire. Garros was showing them how to do it, and he scored two more victories in the following two weeks.

But on April 19, on a raid behind German lines, Garros's engine failed. When he made a forced landing in a meadow surrounded by enemy soldiers, the Germans seized both him and his plane.

German officials sent Garros to a prisoner of war camp. They turned his plane over to Anthony Fokker, a brilliant young Dutch pilot and airplane designer. The Germans had hired Fokker to advise them on plane design and armament.

Fokker thought Garros's deflector device was interesting but crude. As far as Fokker was concerned, the best thing about the deflector was that it motivated him to think about a better way of shooting machine-gun bullets through a propeller.

In short order, Fokker came up with a synchronized propeller system. The system consisted of cranks and rods, which allowed a machine gun to fire only when the propeller blades were horizontal and, therefore, out of the line of a shooting bullet.

In combat, the system was an instant success, working flawlessly for Germany's fleet of planes. Their pilots gunned down almost every French and British plane that dared to challenge them. The Germans thought they were unbeatable in the air.

But it didn't take long for the Allies to capture a downed German plane and copy its synchronized propeller system. By the autumn of 1915, the adjustment had put the Germans and Allied fighter planes on equal technical footing. The battle for supremacy in the skies was about to begin.

In the new age of air warfare, fighter planes had a mix of jobs. They charted the enemy's infantry activity down below. They took photographs of troop movements. They dropped bombs on enemy positions and strafed troops who advanced out of their trenches. But most of all, the fighter planes fought one another for domination in battles above the ground.

Every major nation formed an air force. Among them, Britain, France, and Germany produced by far the best airplanes and the best pilots. Their dogfights in the air – British planes against German planes, French pilots versus German pilots – became the centerpieces of the great air rivalry.

Allied and German fighter pilots emerged as the glamour figures of the war. Everybody who read the newspapers and listened to the radio knew the names of the air aces and the numbers of enemy planes they shot down in their spectacular dogfights.

Oswald Boelcke gave German planes the edge over the Allies in the war's first years. Boelcke was an excellent pilot who had a knack for organizing other German pilots into what he called hunting packs. The packs were made up of anywhere from five or six planes to twenty or thirty. No matter the size, the packs flew in closely drilled teams searching out Allied planes to pick off in the air.

Boelcke emphasized patience. He wanted an exacting style from his pilots, with lots of cooperative work and no acrobatic showing off. Every man in Boelcke's packs was under orders to line up his plane in position for good clean shots at enemy planes. Only then was he allowed to fire his machine gun.

The system worked to perfection, and with Boelcke in charge, the Germans shot down significantly more planes than their Allied counterparts.

For a man who preached caution, Boelcke made one extraordinarily bad error. It happened on October 28, 1916, when he was leading his sixth patrol of the day. The patrol got into a fight with a British squad. Boelcke's plane took a hit, and he was forced to make a crash landing. If only he hadn't forgotten to strap himself into the cockpit, he would have survived the emergency.

Without the strap, which fatigue from the six patrols may have caused him to forget, Boelcke's head struck the front of the cockpit. Just twenty-seven years old, Boelcke had shot down forty Allied planes in his short career. He died in the crash.

Without question, Boelcke's best choice of pilot for his fighting packs was Manfred von Richthofen. An ace among aces, Richthofen became famous as the Red Baron. "Red" came from the bright color of his plane, "Baron" from a title he inherited.

In style, Richthofen stuck to the characteristics that Boelcke demanded. Not at all flamboyant, the Red Baron took no risks. He was unemotional in the air, a cold technician in the cockpit. In numbers of enemy planes downed, no flyer from any air force topped Richthofen: he sent eighty Allied planes crashing from the skies.

On April 30, 1917, the Red Baron and Billy Bishop tangled in the air. They had crossed paths before, but this was their first shooting battle: Bishop and one other Royal Flying Corps Nieuport against Richthofen and three other German Albatroses.

Singling out Bishop, Richthofen came at his Nieuport on a hard right angle while Bishop banked over on his side. Bishop thought Richthofen hadn't a chance of finding a good shot. But Richthofen's bullets ripped into Bishop's fuselage just behind the cockpit, and one bullet pierced the fold in Bishop's flying coat. Bishop considered it the best piece of shooting he'd ever seen.

Richthofen turned and dived again at Bishop. The next burst of the Red Baron's bullets cracked the Nieuport's instrument panel and sent a spray of Bishop's own fuel oil into his face. Bishop was angry with himself for letting the Baron take potshots at him. He pulled into a quick climb, then into an equally swift dive. The maneuver placed him above and behind the Baron's Albatros. Bishop fired from two hundred feet. He felt certain his bullets caught Richthofen's plane.

The Red Baron rolled into a sudden drop toward the ground, Albatros nose pointed down, dark smoke streaming from the tail. For a moment, Bishop thought he had made the ultimate hit on the German ace. But the Baron was faking: the dive was a trick he played often in tight spots, pretending to be in worse shape than he was, gunning his engine to spew smoke from his plane, getting out of his enemy's range.

After dropping four thousand feet, Richthofen leveled his plane and dashed eastward for his home field, leaving Bishop to shake his head at the Red Baron's gimmick. As Richthofen flew away, he waggled his wings at Bishop in a last mocking gesture.

The short encounter on the April day was the only time when Bishop and the Red Baron met in single combat, man to man.

Two months later, in early July 1917, Richthofen was wounded in a dogfight. The wounds brought on nausea and severe headaches, which grounded him for months. When Richthofen returned to the air in October, he seemed no longer the calm, cool operator. The Red Baron had lost his edge.

On April 21, 1918, flying low over a region of the Somme held by Australian troops, Richthofen engaged two planes from the Royal Flying Corps in a dogfight. Struck in the body by a flying bullet during the exchanges, Richthofen barely managed to land his plane in an enemy field.

By the time Australian soldiers reached the downed plane, Richthofen was slumped in the cockpit, dead from the single shot. Since the bullet cut upwards through Richthofen's chest, it had almost certainly been fired from the ground. Further investigation showed that a lucky shot by an Australian machine gunner named Cedric Popkin ended the career of the Red Baron. Richthofen was a month short of his twenty-fifth birthday.

———

Compared to Richthofen and the other German pilots, the British were more independent. They performed strongly enough in teamwork, but they were absolutely brilliant in solo dogfights.

A pioneering British pilot, Lanoe Hawker, planned his attacks with scientific precision. He became expert at positioning himself between the sun and the German plane he targeted. If the German pilot glanced Hawker's way, all he saw was the sun's glare. Then Hawker shot him down.

Hawker scored a modest number of victories – just seven – but they came very early in the air war, making Hawker the first celebrated British pilot. It was his example that alerted the Royal Flying Corps to the full potential of fighter planes. The successes ended for Hawker on November 23, 1916, when Richthofen got the better of him in a dogfight. Lanoe Hawker was the Red Baron's eleventh kill.

Dozens of Royal Flying Corps pilots with dazzling gifts in air combat followed Hawker, finding in him an inspiration.

Mick Mannock was one of the new breed of RFC flyers, a working class youngster and a committed socialist who shot down forty-seven German planes. Albert Ball accounted for almost as many kills, shooting forty-four Germans out of the air. James McCudden, one of three brothers in the RFC, gunned down a remarkable fifty-seven enemy planes.

All three of the aces – Mannock, Ball, and McCudden – died in combat. Each received the Victoria Cross for valor in the air.

By the summer of 1917, the RFC was pulling even with the Germans. The British developed new fighter planes – the Sopwith Camel, the S. E. 5, the Bristol Fighter – that had more speed and easier handling than Germany's latest products.

At the same time, the RFC's pilots were elevating their skills to a level that eventually surpassed the Germans. When Richthofen went down, Germany had dozens of disciplined flyers that made sure victories didn't come easily to the British. Still, pilots such as Mannock, Ball, and McCudden gradually proved their superiority.

Of them all, superb as the British flyers were, no one in the RFC bettered the performance of Canadian Billy Bishop.

———

Bishop wasn't perfect. Fellow pilots kidded him about his terrible landings. He came close to cracking up more than one plane when he bumped to a misjudged landing that shook loose every nut and bolt.

On the plus side, Bishop had fast reflexes and excellent hand-eye coordination. Up in the air, the instant an enemy plane flew into range, Bishop reacted within a split second. In a dogfight, he was the first to fire. Above all, he possessed phenomenally accurate marksmanship. A good shooting eye was a gift he first showed when he was a kid firing his air rifle back in his small hometown of Owen Sound, Ontario.

At the beginning of the war, Bishop joined the Mississauga Horse, then transferred to the Seventh Canadian Mounted Rifles. Both were cavalry units, which suited Bishop with his affection for horseback riding. But after a taste of the rain, mud, and mess of fighting on the ground in France, he changed his mind about the cavalry. He was drawn to the little fighter planes up above, free and clear in the sky. Pilots, Bishop decided, were the only warriors that were masters of their own fate.

He arranged a switch to the Royal Flying Corps – Canada had no air force of its own – where he trained as a pilot. On March 25, 1917, assigned to the RFC's 60th Air Squadron at Filescamp Farm, Bishop announced his arrival by shooting down his first German plane on his first combat flight.

"Today," he wrote that night in a letter to his mother, "I have had the most exciting adventure of my life."

April 1917 brought the hottest air battles of the war. During "Bloody April," as the month came to be called, the RFC lost 151 planes in fierce fights that raged several times a day. The German losses were fewer, with just 119 downed planes. Despite the differences, the pilots of the RFC fought valiantly. They could sense the tide slowly turning in their favor.

Bishop, just coming into his own, put himself in the thick of the April fighting. Although he shot down twelve German planes during the hectic month, the number didn't match the Red Baron's score: Richthofen knocked off twenty-two British planes. But Bishop had begun to make his mark as the best of the RFC pilots.

Throughout the war, Bishop was the man who had luck on his side. While most great fighter pilots, Allied and German, never lived to see the war's end, Bishop survived past 1918 and on for many more decades. He took his share of hits in combat and suffered more than enough injuries and ailments. But he always escaped death in the air.

The French fighter plane hides in the clouds until the pilot spots a German plane to attack down below. (ILN/Mary Evans Picture Library)

Once, in late July 1917, flying low on his return to Filescamp Farm, Bishop's plane was struck by shrapnel from the ground. The Nieuport's nose broke into flames. Smoke filled the cockpit. Feeling disoriented, Bishop just managed to hold the plane in the air until he was over Allied territory. He pointed toward an empty field, but on his way down, he struck a row of poplar trees. The plane broke into pieces, and Bishop was stuck in the wrecked cockpit, hanging upside down, flames licking close to him.

But good fortune was with Bishop. Heavy rain fell from the sky, and while Bishop hung unconscious, the rain put out the flames. When soldiers rescued Bishop, he was shaken, but all in one piece. Two days of rest put him back in flying form.

Not long afterwards, Bishop returned from a dogfight, his plane riddled with bullet holes. After he landed, his mechanic inspected the Nieuport, pulling lightly on the plane's tail. It came off in his hand. If Bishop had flown a minute longer, the tail would have fallen off in the air.

"You're a lucky man," the mechanic said to Bishop.

For the last months of 1917, Bishop was ordered home to Canada, where his fame as a great fighter pilot was used to encourage morale and raise money for the war effort. He hated the fuss and couldn't wait to get back in the air.

When he returned to combat in early 1918, it was as the commander of his own squadron, the 85th. His freshly trained pilots, who were even younger than Bishop's twenty-four years, gave the squadron a happy-go-lucky nickname, the Flying Foxes. Bishop played along with the name by allowing pilots who knocked at least two Germans out of the air to attach foxtails to their wing struts.

To no one's surprise, Bishop emerged as the ace of the 85th. In June 1918, he shot down fifteen German planes in nine days of fighting. To account for the fifteen, Bishop needed a total of just three hundred bullets, about twenty rounds for each enemy he destroyed. It was an astounding show of marksmanship.

Through the whole month of June, Bishop fought at the peak of his talents at the time the RFC showed its dominance over Germany's planes. The Allied flyers were on their way to triumph in the battle for the skies. The victory was one necessary part of the greater victory that the Allies thought was soon to come, when they would crush Germany on the ground.

In the final months of 1918, Bishop was assigned back to Britain, where he trained other Canadian pilots. Although he wasn't in Europe for the last air battles, he had shot down seventy-two German planes. No other pilot in the RFC beat that number, and only Richthofen among the Germans had a higher count. More than any pilot, Billy Bishop showed the way to glory in the air.

11 THE YANKS GO MARCHING IN

GILBERT PARKER, A MEMBER OF BRITAIN'S Parliament, thought the job he agreed to take on in the early weeks of the war sounded difficult, but not impossible. The British government asked Parker to persuade the United States to come into the war to support the Allies.

From the Great War's outbreak, Americans refused to join in the fighting. They said the war was Europe's business, not America's. Woodrow Wilson, the high-minded American president, found war repulsive. "The United States," he said, "is too proud to fight."

In 1916, Wilson offered to act as the middleman in arranging a peace treaty between Germany and the Allies. But he would have nothing to do with combat. The majority of Americans agreed with the president.

Gilbert Parker set out to change their minds.

Born in Canada in 1862, Parker made his fame as the best-selling author of adventure novels featuring swashbuckling French Canadians. The novels attracted

American President Woodrow Wilson refuses to commit his country to war until the Germans provoke the United States into joining the Allies in 1917. (Toronto Reference Library)

hundreds of thousands of readers in the United States and England, turning Parker into an international celebrity. After marrying a wealthy American heiress, he and his wife moved to England, where he was soon elected to Parliament.

In the late summer of 1914, Parker joined the British government's new and secret propaganda wing, whose purpose was to spread the message that the Allied cause was just and that the evil Germans must be defeated at all costs. Word went out from the propaganda people in unsigned newspaper articles and unattributed radio scripts, in publicity pamphlets and in private correspondence.

Nothing identified the material as coming from government sources. The hired writers worked anonymously behind the scenes, keeping up British morale at home and encouraging support in other nations for the Allies fighting in foreign battlefields.

The organization devoted one of its largest departments to the United States, headed by Gilbert Parker. With his American wife and the popularity of his novels there, he made a natural choice.

Parker compiled a list of 260,000 prominent Americans and another list of 555 American newspapers. Then he flooded the mail of the prominent people and the daily papers with stories and personal messages. All of the correspondence carried only Parker's name, with no mention of official Britain. Everything in Parker's stories and letters played up the horrors that the Germans were inflicting on the rest of the world. Parker was making the point that the United States owed it to the Allied countries to join in the fight.

Germany's record of wartime atrocities gave Parker plenty of material to work with.

The destruction of Louvain was one of the first incidents. During Germany's sweep through Belgium in August 1914, ten thousand German soldiers went on a rampage in the ancient university town. The soldiers burned the university's library and its 230,000 rare books. They put torches to the rest of the town's buildings, killed 209 residents, and sent forty thousand more citizens fleeing from the city.

In another event, a German U-boat fired a torpedo at an unarmed British ocean liner named the *Lusitania*. The date was May 7, 1915; the place was the Atlantic Ocean, just off the southern tip of Ireland. The *Lusitania* sank in eighteen minutes, taking 1,198 innocent passengers and crew to their deaths. One hundred and twenty-eight of the dead were Americans.

Almost as shocking was the case of Edith Cavell, an English nurse who ran a clinic in Brussels. A German military court ruled that Cavell was an Allied spy and sentenced her to death. On October 12, 1915, a German firing squad executed Nurse Cavell.

Gilbert Parker felt sure that his accounts of these horrors were convincing the United States of Germany's cruelties. He was giving the Americans every reason to take up the Allied cause. But it wasn't until the episode known as the Zimmerman Telegram that Parker made a breakthrough.

In January 1917, the Germans decided to unleash on Atlantic shipping its fleet of U-boats. While Germany's High Seas Fleet was of little use after the Battle of Jutland, its 150 U-boats remained a threat to the Allies. In 1915 alone, they sank 227 British ships, most of them transporting arms and other goods.

The German plan of early 1917 was to expand the U-boat attacks to include ships of every nation that were carrying cargoes to Britain. Germany intended to blockade Britain and starve it into submission.

Since the United States was the number-one supplier of food and weapons to Britain, American ships would be the prime targets of the U-boat offense. Knowing the United States was bound to be furious, Germany cooked up a scheme to divert American military attention to a different threat.

The scheme involved Mexico, America's neighbor to the south. Germany would promise armed support to Mexico if the Mexicans agreed to invade the United States. The plan seemed perfect to the Germans: Mexico would keep the Americans occupied, and in return, Germany guaranteed that Mexico would be rewarded with the eventual possession of three large American states: Texas, New Mexico, and Arizona.

Arthur Zimmerman, Germany's undersecretary for foreign affairs, took charge of putting the scheme into operation. As a first step, he composed a coded message, which he intended to send to Felix von Eckhardt, the German ambassador in Mexico. The message outlined the invasion plan, and in it, Zimmerman instructed Eckhardt to discuss the idea with Mexico's president in strictest secrecy.

Unfortunately for the Germans, Mexico had no facilities to receive a telegram directly from Germany. Zimmerman's solution to the problem was to direct the telegram to Count Johann Heinrich von Bernstorff, German's ambassador to the United States in Washington. Bernstorff would relay the details of Zimmerman's message in a telegram of his own to Eckhardt in Mexico.

On January 15, Zimmerman fired off his coded telegram to Bernstorff by way of three different cable stations. One station was located in the American embassy in Berlin, the second in Sweden's Berlin embassy, and the third on Long Island in New York State.

Unknown to Zimmerman, the alert cryptologists of Room 40 in London intercepted all three telegrams.

The code in the telegrams turned out to be tricky, but in a few days, a smart young Room 40 operative named Nigel de Grey led the way in cracking Zimmerman's message. As de Grey and the other cryptologists read the decoded telegrams, they recognized the bombshell they held in their hands. When the Americans learned what the Germans planned, they would surely be shaken into declaring war on Germany.

But Room 40 had a reservation. If Britain took the telegram to the Americans, the Germans would realize that the British were intercepting and decoding all of their messages. Britain's cover for its cryptology operation would be blown.

Room 40 came up with a way around the problem. What they needed was a copy of the telegram from Ambassador Bernstorff in Washington to Ambassador Eckhardt in Mexico City. If they took a decoded copy of this telegram to the Americans, then the Germans would conclude that the leak took place in Washington or Mexico City, not in London.

By luck and good espionage, British intelligence agents obtained a copy of the Bernstorff telegram. On February 20, the agents delivered the copy to Room 40, where everybody had one more doubt. What if the Americans thought the British cryptologists had made up the whole thing? What if the Americans believed Room 40 faked the telegram and the decoding?

To head off this possibility, the man in charge of Room 40, Admiral William Hall, took Nigel de Grey and the undecoded version of the Bernstorff telegram to the American embassy in London. While embassy officials watched, de Grey went through the entire decoding process once again. The astounded Americans became instant believers in the telegram's veracity.

On February 24, British Foreign Secretary Arthur Balfour sent a copy of the decoded telegram to President Woodrow Wilson.

A week later, Gilbert Parker began a blitz of his 260,000 prominent Americans and 555 American newspapers with the news of Germany's treachery. Parker piled on the pressure through all of March, arguing that America could never trust Germany, that Germany presented a menace to the United States that only a war could drive away. Parker thought his argument was working.

On April 6, 1917, the United States declared war on Germany.

To command the new American military force, President Wilson chose a strong-willed general named John J. Pershing. A personal tragedy had already tested Pershing. In August 1915, while he was away from home leading a campaign against Mexican bandits on the border between the United States and Mexico, a fire in his house at an army base in northern California took the lives of his wife and three young daughters. Only his six-year-old son, Warren, survived. Stoic and resilient, Pershing soldiered on.

On May 28, 1917, Pershing sailed for Europe on the *Baltic* with 191 officers and soldiers. Britain heaved a sigh of relief at having the United States committed to the fight. France was even happier. With half of the French Army in mutiny, France's generals worried that the Germans might attempt to break through the weakened French lines. The generals cheered up at the prospect that the Americans were on their way to the Western Front: American soldiers would fill the gaps left by the mutinying troops.

On June 13, when Pershing reached Paris by train, the Parisians went wild with joy. The crowd greeting Pershing was so large and boisterous that he needed an hour to drive the two miles to his hotel. Paris's people sensed a turning point in the war.

But French jubilation was premature. As the small size of Pershing's advance party hinted, the United States wasn't close to being ready for battle. At the time America declared war, it hadn't fought in major combat since its own Civil War in the 1860s. The U.S. army of 1917 consisted of no more than one hundred thousand soldiers. The country's best-trained military men served in the elite Marine Corps, but the corps was only fifteen thousand strong.

Marching down a broad Parisian avenue, these American soldiers, fresh off a ship, arrive in time for the war's last battles. (ILN/Mary Evans Picture Library)

The total number of available American fighters was too small to make a difference in the battles on the Western Front. They wouldn't be filling gaps in the French lines anytime soon. The French generals grew impatient and irritable, and through the rest of the war, they could never quite bring themselves to give the Americans their full respect.

In a Herculean effort of patriotism, America started from scratch to build an army that would meet their obligations as a declared enemy of Germany. The American government put a draft in place, conscripting men of military age into the armed services. The new soldiers trained in army camps set up all over the United States. It took months to instruct these raw recruits in the lessons of warfare, and it wasn't until late in 1917 that American soldiers began to reach Europe in numbers that mattered.

By the spring of 1918, about three hundred thousand soldiers from the United States were settled into positions behind the Western Front. And by early August, another million American soldiers swelled their ranks.

In October of 1917, four battalions from the earliest U.S. contingent went into the trenches near Nancy, in northern France. They were to serve under French command, a baptism in battle for the American troops.

But things went wrong from the first day. It was chilly autumn weather, with icy rain falling. The Americans wore summer uniforms because an army bureaucrat in Washington told Pershing that the warm woolen uniforms were needed for the draftees back home. In the Nancy trenches, the soldiers in light clothing came down with miserable colds.

German shells battered the American position. An American lieutenant, in charge of his brigade, called for a French counter-barrage. The French officer overseeing the Americans disagreed. Oozing condescension, the Frenchman said he knew better than this naïve young American lieutenant: there would be no counter-barrage.

A few days later, two hundred German infantrymen stormed into the American trenches. For fifteen minutes, the Americans resisted the Germans in hand-to-hand combat. With no room to fire rifles, both sides fought with every weapon within reach: knives, spades, hammers.

Fortunately for the Americans, the casualties in this awkward and free-form battle were small. The Germans killed just three Americans, wounded five others, and left with a dozen prisoners. On the American side, the soldiers killed two

German attackers and wounded five others. It was a fierce and ugly introduction to warfare in the Western Front style.

The fight at Nancy, small and insignificant as it might seem in the war's larger picture, nevertheless confirmed for General Pershing a conclusion he had already reached: the United States must fight as an American army under American command.

The French and British scoffed at Pershing's idea. Officers from France and Britain, dismissive of America's fighting abilities at this stage of the war, thought the American troops were more useful as replacement units, filling in for French and British forces that needed rest, or had suffered heavy casualties. Under all circumstances, the American troops would answer to French and British commanders.

Pershing soon realized that American soldiers needed to impress the European officers with their performance in the field. The French and British had been

The officer without the hat, studying the lines where the Germans are soon to attack near the French town of Saint-Quentin, is General John Pershing, commander of the American troops. (ILN/Mary Evans Picture Library)

fighting the war since the summer of 1914. Only through success on the battlefield could the American fighting men, newcomers to the war, prove to the Europeans that the United States deserved a separate army under American leadership.

In early June 1918, when American troops were reaching the Western Front in substantial numbers, a brigade of the U.S. Marine Corps served under the French in a hectic fight near Rheims, in northeastern France.

Determined to battle to the death, the Germans threw a tremendous barrage of artillery and infantry at the French position. The French officers decided on a strategic retreat: they would pull back, regroup their men, then press forward again.

The French summoned the American officer in charge of the Marines, Captain Lloyd Williams. The Marines had been successfully resisting the German attempt to seize a key road leading towards Rheims. The French told Captain Williams they were going into retreat and the Marines should do the same.

"Retreat?" Williams answered. "Hell, we just got here!"

The Marines continued to fight for the road to Rheims. Later in the day, a French counterattack drove the Germans into retreat.

As Captain Williams showed in his unique style, the American soldiers had grown beyond eager to show their worth as fighters. Gradually, the French and British were coming around to Pershing's view of an independent army. So many hundreds of thousands of U.S. troops had reached Europe by August 1918 that not even the most snobbish French officer could deny the Americans a right to an army of their own.

The timing for France's change of heart couldn't have been better. Through the summer of 1918, the Germans were preparing for a final drive against the Allies. It was an offensive that would decide the war's outcome. At this strategically essential moment, the American Army at last took its place alongside the other Allied armies.

12 LAST BATTLES

GENERAL ERICH LUDENDORFF HAD A miserable fifty-second birthday. Ludendorff was the German officer who made his reputation as a tactician in the routing of the Belgians at Liège and in the defeat of the Russians at Tannenberg in 1914. He continued to lead the armies on the Eastern Front until August 1916, when the kaiser promoted him to the command of the entire Western Front.

In his new post, Ludendorff worked in partnership with General Paul von Hindenburg, who was almost twenty years older and superior in rank. Despite Hindenburg's seniority, he allowed Ludendorff to take the lead. Whenever Hindenburg was asked his opinion about a plan or a battle, he turned to Ludendorff and said, "What do you think?" Germany's fate in the war would rise or fall on Ludendorff's instincts and nerve.

On Ludendorff's fifty-second birthday, his nerve took a bad hit. It was April 9, 1917, the day the Canadians captured Vimy Ridge. Until then, Ludendorff

In the last year of the war, Germany's fate depends on the leadership of these two imposing generals, Paul von Hindenburg (left) and Erich Ludendorff. (ILN/Mary Evans Picture Library)

doubted the Allies could break the German lines at any point along the Western Front. The Canadians proved him wrong.

That evening, Hindenburg visited Ludendorff's office to wish him a happy birthday. He found Ludendorff deflated over the Vimy defeat.

"We've known worse times," Hindenburg said, trying to cheer up his colleague. But later, alone with his journal, Hindenburg wrote, "The impact of the news throws a somber picture – much shade, little light."

Ludendorff worked eighteen hours a day, leaving little time for family or pleasures while he mapped out strategies to win the war. If the German cause were lost, he would be the first to realize it. While Vimy shook him, Ludendorff was still convinced his armies could overcome the Allies in the long run.

Throughout 1917, Ludendorff bided his time. He planned no big offensive actions for the year, putting off his grand attack until 1918. While he waited, he set about the business of reinforcing his army.

In the autumn of 1917, Ludendorff took a role in arranging the treaty with Vladimir Lenin's Bolshevik government in Russia. With the end of the fight

French soldiers have just completed a successful counterattack against the Germans, who can be seen in retreat on the horizon. (ILN/Mary Evans Picture Library)

against the Russian Army, fifty divisions of German soldiers were freed from duties on the Eastern Front.

Ludendorff brought the men home and prepared them for the battle on the Western Front. At the time, he had no other source of fresh troops: every German male, except for the very young and the very old, had already been conscripted into the war. Ludendorff looked on the one million soldiers from the east as his salvation.

Ludendorff could wait no longer than early spring of 1918 to launch a do-or-die offensive. He had to make his move before the millions of arriving American soldiers were ready for battle. Ludendorff's own army, beefed up with the Eastern Front soldiers, would never be stronger than it was that spring. He fixed March 21 as the date for the first offensive.

The point of attack was to be the French town of Saint-Quentin, on the edge of the Somme region. British troops defended the area, though their numbers weren't nearly equal to the army that Ludendorff massed in the German trenches.

Ludendorff's plan was to break through the British strongholds on a straight line that, with good fortune and determined fighting, would carry the Germans all the way to the English Channel. Once there, they could cut off the British Army's supply sources. The chances of taking France would then swing in Germany's favor.

Before sunrise on March 21, German artillery blasted a sudden barrage at the British.

Along with the artillery, the Germans released three different poison gases. Chlorine would turn a soldier's face blue and fill his lungs with enough water to drown in. Phosgene caused the lungs to discharge pints of sickening yellow liquid. And mustard gas blistered the skin and made the victim cough up mucous membrane.

Gas masks rescued most of the British at Saint-Quentin from this horrible fate. Early in the war, soldiers had no protection from gas except handkerchiefs soaked in water. Fairly quickly, Britain's scientists developed miniature respirators, which fit into odd-looking masks with large goggles to see through. These contraptions saved the majority of soldiers in the Saint-Quentin attack, although the gas still took many men's lives and drove many others to flee from their trenches.

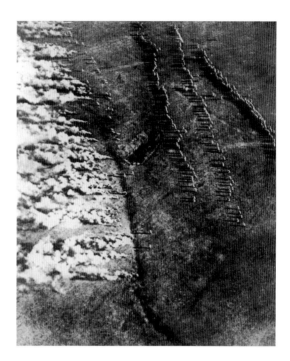

The thick white floating cloud on the left is poison gas. The Germans unleash it on a British position in the hours before they attack in March 1918.
(ILN/Mary Evans Picture Library)

At 9:40 that morning, March 21, after the German artillery and poison gases finished their work, the infantry attacked. Seventy-six German divisions were matched against twenty-eight British divisions along a front of fifty miles.

Coming at the outnumbered British in a whirlwind of furious fighting, the Germans easily broke the enemy lines. They rushed ahead so quickly that they took twenty-one thousand British prisoners on the first day. The desperate British fought back, but they couldn't stop the Germans that day, or in further attacks in the next five days.

Back in Berlin, the kaiser was in ecstasy. On March 23, he gave German children a day off school, calling it a victory holiday.

In the Saint-Quentin fighting, the Germans advanced a quick twenty miles. Then, in early April, just as the attack seemed to be proceeding triumphantly, it bogged down. A stiffening in the British resistance was one reason; German battle fatigue was another. And a third was the condition of the Somme region, where the fighting took place. With its massive clutter from past battles, the Somme made tough terrain to struggle through. The shelled fields, ruined roads, and networks of wrecked trenches slowed the Germans to a crawl.

With persistence, the German drive to the English Channel might yet have worked. But Ludendorff suddenly shut it down. On the spur of the moment, acting mostly on instinct, he decided to change tactics. His new plan was to attack the British at a point to the north of Saint-Quentin.

On April 9, Ludendorff made sure that his fifty-third birthday was happier than his fifty-second had been. There would be no repeat of a setback like the one at Vimy Ridge. Instead, Ludendorff celebrated by launching his second offensive of the spring, with a fierce artillery bombardment against the British on either side of the French border with Belgium.

The heavy assault alarmed Douglas Haig, the British commander in chief who had been promoted to field marshal on January 1, 1917. More worried than at any time in the war, he wrote a frantic memo telling his officers that they had their backs to the wall. Haig begged every man to fight to the end.

The field marshal's plea didn't get the result he counted on. His uninspired troops were driven back by the German infantry, which gained steadily. But again, just as things seemed to be going so right for Ludendorff, the battle soon followed the pattern of the Saint-Quentin fight.

While the German lines advanced by several miles, it wasn't as far as Ludendorff wanted. And the casualties rose too high. Ludendorff lost 120,000 soldiers – men he couldn't replace. Germany hadn't a single soldier to spare, and Ludendorff could little afford to take chances with the lives of the men still under his command.

On April 29, he ended the offensive.

Rallying once more, Ludendorff decided on a third offensive. He would tackle the French section of the Western Front south of the British lines. An advance down the valley of the Oise River could put the Germans on course for Paris, just ninety miles away. The thought of capturing Paris picked up Ludendorff's spirits.

He began the offensive on May 27 with the familiar artillery barrage, but this one was different: it packed more stupendous power than the others. In four hours, six thousand German guns fired two million shells.

Then the German infantry attacked.

The battle continued off and on into the summer. German soldiers made sufficient progress for Ludendorff to imagine that Paris was within his grasp. But as the days went by, he became apprehensive. Ludendorff recognized problems were rising that could doom the offensive.

His soldiers' morale was plummeting. As the men made advances, capturing positions that the French and British had occupied for months, the German soldiers were angered when they saw their enemies' living spaces and food supplies. They realized that ordinary British and French soldiers were much better off than they were.

Four years of shortages in Germany brought on by Allied blockades meant that German soldiers got by each day on tiny portions of potatoes and moldy bread. Compared to these meager meals, the British and French appeared to have dined like kings, and the German soldiers felt cheated. They began to lose motivation for continuing the fight.

The army's discontent worried Ludendorff, and so did the prospect of facing the fresh and enthusiastic Americans.

Ludendorff had his first disturbing encounter with troops from the United States when two American divisions served with the French in resisting the latest German offensive. In early June, a brigade of U.S. Marines counterattacked at a place called Belleau Wood. The struggle over the mile-wide forest lasted twenty days. It cost the Marines five thousand men in casualties, but they stuck to the fight and captured their objective.

The Americans were tougher than Ludendorff imagined. They came to the battles without the weariness and cynicism that the German troops were feeling after four years of the endless war. Ludendorff knew that millions more idealistic Americans would soon get into the fight against his army. The thought made his heart sink.

On August 8, an Allied force made up of British, Australian, and Canadian soldiers cracked through the German lines at the Somme. In raids that Ludendorff hadn't anticipated, the Allies took back the territory that the Germans had seized in the March fighting.

Leading with their bayonets, British soldiers make prisoners of the German troops hiding in a dugout. (ILN/Mary Evans Picture Library)

Ludendorff couldn't believe the news of the latest setback. On top of his other problems, events at the Somme were the final blow. Ludendorff flew into a rage, shouting and ranting behind the closed door of his office. When he pulled himself together, he went to Hindenburg's office. He told Hindenburg that an armistice with the Allies was Germany's only choice.

"August 8," Ludendorff said, still seething with anger, "is the black day of the German Army."

Two days later, meeting with the kaiser, Ludendorff repeated what he had said to Hindenburg. The kaiser was flabbergasted. Such a shocking end to the war had never entered his mind.

Germany could expect no help from its two partners, Turkey and the Austro-Hungarian Empire.

As warriors, the Turks peaked during the fight to protect Gallipoli. After that, their fortunes headed straight downhill. Losing battles against the Russians in the Caucasus Mountains drained Turkey of men and energy. Parts of the Arab empire it ruled for centuries, the Ottoman Empire, were sliced away by British troops. Turkey lost all motive for war, and by the summer of 1918, it wanted nothing more than an armistice.

The Austro-Hungarian Empire, shaky at the beginning of the war, grew weaker and more fractured each year. Field Marshal Conrad von Hotzendorf, the army's chief of staff, thought in early 1918 that his men could at least defeat the Italians to his south. But when French and British troops propped up Italy's army, the Austro-Hungarians suffered yet another loss. Hotzendorf, once the most confident general in all of Europe, was kicked out of his job.

As the Empire reeled from their military failures, its people took advantage of the turmoil to break away and form their own nations. The Slavs, Croats, and Slovenes recreated themselves as Yugoslavia. The Czechs and Slovaks announced the formation of an independent republic, Czechoslovakia. And the Poles regained their independence.

The Austro-Hungarian Empire crashed, and none of the countries that emerged from the wreckage was interested in fighting a war.

General Ludendorff got a grip on himself. After the meltdown of August 8, he decided to take a completely different course – a strong defense to save the day.

Ludendorff ordered the German troops up and down the Western Front to fall back to an established line that roughly followed the arc of the autumn 1914 German positions. Named the Hindenburg Line after Ludendorff's colleague, the new line made a vantage point for Ludendorff to set up his still-powerful artillery. The Germans would bombard the attacking Allies, then blitz them with local counterattacks.

Ludendorff's plan ran into trouble almost before he put it into action.

On September 12, south of Verdun, General John Pershing and his American troops attacked the Germans in an area called Saint-Mihiel. It was the first time the Americans fought as an army on their own. The attack caught the Germans just as they were packing for the fallback to the Hindenburg Line.

As the battle progressed, the Americans appeared not to be sophisticated fighters, not even efficient soldiers. But they were keen, and that was enough. In just one day of battle, American soldiers took thirteen thousand German prisoners and captured 450 of their heavy guns.

A few days later, sensing an unmistakable turn in the tide of the war, the French Army's chief of staff, Marshal Ferdinand Foch, issued a simple but stirring call to arms to his fellow Allied commanders: "Everyone to battle!"

On September 26, in an immense assault of 250,00 men – the armies of Britain, France, Belgium, the United States, and Canada – fractured holes in the German positions along the Hindenburg Line. The German soldiers, beleaguered as they were, refused to quit. But the Allies were in no mood to let enemy resistance get in their way: they rolled over the German opposition.

Ludendorff threw another temper tantrum, raging against the people he considered responsible for the new defeat. The list included just about everybody except himself. He told Hindenburg that an armistice was the only option.

Ludendorff soon changed his mind. In early October, he announced that armistice was out of the question and that he and the army would fight on.

But this time, German opinion turned against him. Sick of the war, the German people and politicians thought Ludendorff was right when he talked of armistice and wrong when he preached continuing resistance. Few of them had the heart for more fighting. They wanted an end to the killing of their young men, no matter what the cost to Germany's image as a superior power.

The soldiers in the straggling line are Germans captured by the British in the battle over the ruined city of Ypres in 1918. (ILN/Mary Evans Picture Library)

The kaiser didn't share his country's general view, but he couldn't ignore the wishes of those around him. As one major concession, he agreed to replace his chancellor, the highest position in the German government. For most of the war years, a fervent military champion named Count Georg von Hertling held the job.

On October 3, the kaiser appointed the much more moderate Prince Max of Baden as his new chancellor. Prince Max, a high-ranking officer in the German Red Cross, had already made it clear he favored a negotiated peace with the Allies.

Prince Max recognized Ludendorff as the obstacle in his way on the path to peace. While the prince thought Germany must pursue the earliest possible opportunity, Ludendorff insisted on getting back to the fight. Prince Max demanded that the kaiser choose between Ludendorff and himself.

On October 26, 1918, the kaiser met with Ludendorff in Berlin. Under pressure, Ludendorff offered his resignation. The kaiser accepted it, saying nothing to thank Ludendorff for his war service.

As Ludendorff walked back to his hotel, he saw the end of Germany as he knew it drawing near. At the hotel, he talked to his wife.

"In two weeks," he said, "there will be no kaiser left, you will see."

While Prince Max and other civilian and military authorities in Berlin organized their negotiations for peace, German troops continued to fight hard. Until an armistice was arrived at, their orders were to defend their own border. Fierce battles broke out, particularly along the front in Belgium. Men died and suffered wounds. The fight went on, even though everyone knew that an agreement for peace was just days away.

On November 4, a British officer named Wilfred Owen led his unit from the Manchester Regiment in an attack on the resisting Germans near the Sambre-Oise Canal. Owen had spent much of the previous year recovering from shell shock at the Craiglockhart Military Hospital in Scotland. A beginning poet, writing antiwar verse, he'd shown his work to another Craiglockhart patient, Siegfried Sassoon. Sassoon looked on Owen as a poet of great promise.

At the age of twenty-five, Wilfred Owen died in battle, cut down by German machine-gun fire at the Sambre-Oise Canal.

After the war, Sassoon edited and published Owen's poetry, which came to be regarded as the classics of the Great War.

The armistice took effect at eleven o'clock on November 11, 1918. The war was over.

Wilhelm II of Germany was safely in neutral Holland. Two days earlier, he had abdicated, stepping down as kaiser. The timing made Ludendorff exactly right in his prediction.

A few hours after the abdication, Wilhelm and a small entourage traveled by train from German Army headquarters to the Dutch town of Doorn. The first thing he did on arrival was ask for a cup of good English tea. He drank the tea, then moved into the local castle, where he lived in comfortable exile until his death twenty-three years later.

As the sign on this Toronto home announces, a soldier has returned safely to his family at the end of the war. The homecoming is a scene repeated millions of times in all the countries whose men served in the war and survived the killing. (City of Toronto Archives, Fonds 1244, Item 904)

Two million German soldiers died in the war. One million, seven hundred French were killed and about the same number of Russians. One million soldiers from Britain and its Dominions died, a million and a half Austro-Hungarians, and hundreds of thousands of Turks.

More than six million young men perished on the battlefields of Europe. The majority were not yet out of their teens or just entering their twenties. They were a generation of lost men, and their deaths became the legacy of the Great War.

AFTERWORD

One corporal from Germany's army who survived the fighting was an Austrian citizen living in the German city of Munich at the start of the war. He joined up in early August 1914, eager to fight for German supremacy. The corporal was wounded at the Battle of the Somme, suffered from the effects of gas in the last battles at Ypres, and was awarded an Iron Cross. He came away from the war with a lust for revenge against the enemies that had inflicted defeat on Germany. The angry corporal's name was Adolf Hitler.

Hitler's message of vengeance resonated first with bitter German army veterans, then with a broad German public. Germany resented the terms imposed by the 1919 Treaty of Versailles, which the victorious Allies drew up. The treaty disarmed the Germans, handed Alsace-Lorraine back to France, and forced economic hardships on Germany. Hitler, a demagogue with frantic charisma, stirred his countrymen's resentment and preached again the kaiser's old beliefs in German world superiority.

In September 1939, Germany, with Hitler as its leader, once again took the world into war. Virtually the same nations that had fought the war from 1914 to 1918 now endured another long and brutal fight. The Second World War lasted until 1945, and far more than the number of soldiers who had died in the First World War were killed before the Allies once again succeeded.

The Second World War grew out of conditions left behind by the First World War. But the need to battle through another universal conflict in no way diminished the sacrifices and accomplishments of the soldiers who fought the earlier war. Looking back, the men of the Great War emerged as figures of even greater gallantry.

SELECTED BIBLIOGRAPHY

Allen, Ralph. *Ordeal by Fire*. Doubleday. 1961.

Barker, Pat. *Regeneration*. Penguin Books. 1991.

Barnwell, Cornelli. *The Swordbearers: Supreme Command in World War I*. Indiana University Press. 1963.

Barris, Ted. *Victory at Vimy: Canada Comes of Age*. Thomas Allen. 2007.

Berton, Pierre. *Vimy*. McClelland & Stewart. 1986.

Bishop, William Arthur. *The Courage of the Early Morning: The True Story of Canada's Flying Hero, Billy Bishop*. McClelland & Stewart. 1965.

Budiansky, Stephen. *Battle of Wits: The Complete Story of Codebreaking*. The Free Press. 2000.

Fleming, Thomas. *The Illusion of Victory: America in World War I*. Basic Books. 2003.

Freeman, Bill, and Nielsen, Richard. *Far From Home: Canadians in the First World War*. McGraw Hill Ryerson. 1999.

Gilbert, Martin. *The Battle of the Somme: The Heroism and Horror of War*. McClelland & Stewart. 2006.

Godefroy, A. B. *For Freedom and Honour: The Story of the 25 Soldiers Executed in the Great War*. CEF Books. 1998.

Gwyn, Sandra. *Tapestry of War*. HarperCollins. 1992.

Holmes, Richard. *Tommy: The British Soldiers on the Western Front.* HarperCollins. 2004.

Keegan, John. *The First World War.* Albert A. Knopf. 1998.

Lippenhahn, Rudolf. *Code Breaking.* Overlook. 1999.

Macfarlane, David. *The Danger Tree.* Macfarlane Walter & Ross. 1991.

Major, Kevin. *No Man's Land.* Doubleday Canada. 1995.

Massie, Robert K. *Dreadnought: Britain, Germany and the Coming of the Great War.* Random House. 1991.

Norris, Geoffrey. *The Royal Flying Corps: A History.* Muller. 1965.

Stacey, A. J. *Memoirs of a Blue Puttee: The Newfoundland Regiment in World War One.* DRC Publishers. 2002.

Strachan, Hew. *The First World War.* Viking. 2004.

Taylor, John W. R. *A History of Aerial Warfare.* Hamlyn. 1974.

Tuchman, Barbara W. *The Guns of August.* Random House. 1962.

ACKNOWLEDGMENTS

Several historians, amateur and professional, who have a particular fascination with the Great War were kind and generous in lending me books from their libraries. I'm more than grateful to Michael and Honor de Pencier, Gary Smith, Ross Fletcher, Peter Smith, and Kathy and Ray Johnson. I owe huge thanks as well to Sarah Batten and Chris Harris; to Sue Tate, Kathy Lowinger, and all the great people at Tundra; and, as always, to Marjorie Harris.

INDEX